· THE IRRESISTIBLE ·

· CHOCOLATE CAKE BOOK ·

· ALSO BY ·
· PAMELLA ASQUITH ·

*The Quintessential Croissant*

*Pamella Z. Asquith's Fruit Tart Cookbook*

PAMELLA ASQUITH

# THE IRRESISTIBLE CHOCOLATE CAKE BOOK

SOUVENIR PRESS

First published in the U.S.A. by
Holt, Rinehart and Winston

First British Edition published 1984 by
Souvenir Press Ltd, 43 Great Russell Street, London WC1B 3PA



ISBN 0 285 62666 3

Design by Amy Hill
Photographs by Marshall Berman
Illustrations by Michael Starkman

Printed in Great Britain by
Richard Clay (The Chaucer Press) Ltd.,
Bungay, Suffolk

• TO MELANIE •

# · CONTENTS ·

# · ACKNOWLEDGMENTS ·

I want to thank the following people for their inspiration and support: Robert Cooperstein, Joyce Cole, Madame Lili, Judy Knipe, Marshall Berman, Michael Starkman, Jane Currant, Kimberley Thompson, Annie Cashion, Tony, Mary, Ariel, and Flora, Adelle and Tita, Jennifer Josephy, and of course, my mother (by default), whose dislike of cooking kept her out of the kitchen long enough for her mischievous daughter to be caught in the middle of a mess, when Mother would always exclaim, "What are you doing NOW!!?"

# • INTRODUCTION •

I do not remember at what age I brought my first chocolate cake into the world, although I will never forget the excitement and pride I felt on presenting it. I must have been seven or eight—old enough to read and follow directions by myself on the cake mix box. Over the years, my techniques and palate have become more sophisticated, but my love of chocolate has never left me.

Bold and experimental, by age seventeen I was not content with making plain gingerbread houses. Having seen the Frank Lloyd Wright houses near my home in the Chicago suburbs, I was determined to make a cantilevered cake. Enlisting the services of an engineering student, I was able to work the design out on paper. Of course, the cake flopped (literally) and achieved infamy as the Frank Lloyd Wrong cake. I had intended to decorate it in the austere manner of Mondrian. Instead, I improvised the Jackson Pollock style to the dismay of my poor mother, who found splashes of brightly colored buttercream in strange places for weeks thereafter.

I was twenty when I got my first job as a pastry chef in a restaurant in Madison, Wisconsin, where I was studying the history of art at the university. I knew nothing of professional pastry-making techniques at the time but my enthusiasm made up for my lack of technical expertise. Then another restaurant in Madison hired me to be not only pastry chef but the one and only cook at lunch and dinner. I managed to fake my way through the main courses only by virtue of the dazzling desserts I turned out. During my two-year tenure I actually did learn to prepare food other than desserts and had ample time and an appreciative audience upon whom to experiment with pastries.

After receiving my degree in the history of art, I departed for sunny California, where I worked at a French bakery in Oakland, whose *propriétaire*, Madame Lili, filled the gaps in my eclectic culinary education and forced me to do it "right." Madame Lili, despite her perfectionism, always allowed me creative freedom, and her graciousness and love of life have been an inspiration. Even after several years we still celebrated each batch of the magical genoise and grieved over earthquake-shattered tortes.

Although I eat most of the pastries I make, I do not weigh two hundred pounds. (My apron strings must be wrapped twice around my middle.) It is inconceivable to me that anyone could do such physically demanding work as pastry making and be overweight. I never have become disenchanted with chocolate or pastry, although for years I have been surrounded by them. (I must admit, however, that once around Easter, I dreamt I was a chocolate bunny attacked by chocolate eggs.) So, dear reader, have no fear of being transformed into a chocolate blimp by merely possessing and using this book; contrary to popular myth, one must actually eat chocolate, not just think about it or make it, in order to gain weight.

Anyone attempting a discussion of cake making is inevitably confronted with having to define what a cake is and when or if a cake is a torte, a gâteau, a torta, a kugel, a gugel, and so on and on. Being a California eclectic, I delight in the linguistic confusion that results from cultures crossing and have named my cakes accordingly.

Perhaps there are some people who do not like chocolate cake. This book is not for them. For the rest, let us proceed with a few words about ingredients, equipment, and techniques. Then on to the recipes and the glorious potential of the simple brown bean.

# HOW TO USE THIS BOOK

## NOTES FOR BRITISH READERS

Since this book originated in the United States (under the title *The Ultimate Chocolate Cake Book*) some of the terms and ingredients used may be unfamiliar to British readers.

The following notes are intended to clarify any points that may cause confusion:

*Baking Pans*—in the United Kingdom these are commonly known as cake tins or baking tins. *Jelly-roll pans* correspond to swiss-roll tins.

*Cake Flour*—this fine, starchy flour has no direct equivalent in the United Kingdom. Advice on achieving the same effect is given on page 13 of this book.

*Chocolate Chestnut Bonbons*—rich American sweets used in the recipe on page 188. They are obtainable in this country in some high-class confectioners' or department stores.

*Macadamia Nuts*—an expensive Hawaiian gourmet nut, similar in appearance to a large hazelnut, obtainable from some whole-food shops.

*Packed*—a term used throughout the book, meaning that the ingredients being measured should be packed tightly into the container.

*Pastry flour*—used in the recipe on page 193; an alternative is given in the list of ingredients.

Throughout the book ingredients are measured in cups, with equivalent ounces in brackets. For convenience, since American standard measures differ from those in Britain, conversion tables showing British Imperial and metric equivalents are given at the end of the book.

Oven temperatures are given throughout in Fahrenheit. A table of gas "regulo" settings is provided at the end of the book.

The recipes in this book are very simple and often are in exact mathematical ratios. Measurement by weight, not volume, is strongly recommended. As the metric system seems to be meeting resistance in the United States, the weight measurements are in the pound/ounce system (although I personally measure metrically). Ingredients are extremely temperature sensitive. Because the recipes in this book (with one exception) do not call for chemical leavening, the cook must be exact as to measurement, temperature of ingredients, and proper technique. Baking is not like making soup; one does not add ingredients to taste. Always assemble all ingredients before proceeding to put together any batter.

Specific methods for such procedures as melting chocolate and beating egg whites are presented in "Professional Tips and Secrets," pages 39–74, rather than with every recipe. Read this section carefully; successful cake making is often more a matter of technique than recipe.

Most of the recipes are original creations. My personal distaste for chemical leavening, flavor extracts, and an overabundance of sugar led me to revise many well-known recipes, and the wonderful selection of fruit available in California and many other parts of the country inspired me to invent new cakes.

Titling a work the "ultimate" anything is presumptuous. I believe I may safely assert that never before has such a range of chocolate cakes been presented between two covers, although I am not fool enough to suppose that this can be the ultimate expression of chocolate's versatility. Even now, surveying the contents of this book other possibilities leap to mind: Chocolate-Praline Cake, Chocolate Persimmon Torte, Maple-Walnut Chocolate Charlotte . . . No doubt this book will inspire many new chocolate confections.

A word of caution: As the cakes in this book are very rich and intense in flavor, a large number of small servings is specified.

# INGREDIENTS

# • CHOCOLATE •

Doubtless the Lord could have made a better bean, but he never did. Indeed, *Theobroma cacao*, the botanical name for the tree from which chocolate and cocoa are derived, means "food of the gods." But any chocolate-lover knows that the bean comes to us in several dramatically altered forms.

Chocolate for baking is generally sold as "unsweetened," "extra-bittersweet," "bittersweet," "semisweet," and "sweet." Unsweetened chocolate, made only from ground cocoa beans, is not as refined or "conched" (kneaded by machine for up to several days) as sweetened chocolate and, therefore, not as smooth or fine tasting. It usually has an emulsifier added. Inferior brands of unsweetened chocolate sometimes simply will not melt; when heated, however carefully, the chocolate turns into a pasty, rubbery, muddy mass.

Other chocolates for baking contain various amounts of added sugar and cocoa butter. They are refined and conched, with "extra-bittersweet" having the least amount of added sugar and "sweet" having the most. However, what one brand labels "bittersweet" may be similar to another brand's "extra-bittersweet" or "semisweet." There is no standard.

Fine European products often list the amounts of cocoa solids and sugar on the package. Of course, the higher the amount of cocoa solids, and the more it is conched, the better the product. For instance, a Swiss brand, Lindt Extra-Bittersweet, contains at least 59 percent cocoa solids. In the United States the minimum amount of cocoa solids required for a chocolate to be termed "bittersweet" is 35 percent. If you assume that most manufacturers comply only with the minimum requirements, it is obvious why fine-quality chocolate often costs more. Cocoa solids are more expensive than sugar, and conching is an expensive, time-consuming process.

As a professional, I have used many fine brands of chocolate, domestic and European, but unfortunately they are not available to the public on a retail level; the top brands of baking chocolate available in retail stores are Lindt, Tobler, Ghirardelli, Guittard, Krön, Callebaut, and Godiva. Lindt and Tobler are Swiss brands, but they are widely imported and generally available in gourmet shops and some supermarkets across the country. Callebaut is from Belgium and is available by mail order. Ghirardelli and Guittard (San Francisco–based companies), Krön (a New York–based company), and Godiva (a recent Belgian transplant) are the only domestic brands that can be compared to the fine Swiss and Belgian companies (see Mail Order Guide, page 229).

"Coating chocolate," "fondant chocolate," or "courverture" is a highly refined chocolate with a lot of cocoa butter added. It has a beautiful patina and makes a shiny buttercream and glaze, but it is generally used more by candy makers than bakers. To my knowledge, it is impossible to obtain this chocolate except by mail order. Always inquire before you order whether the so-called coating chocolate has vegetable fat added instead of cocoa butter, and do not buy it if it does. "Coating chocolate" can be used for baking, but reduce the butter or cream (or other fats) in the recipe by 10 percent to compensate for the additional fat in the chocolate itself.

"White chocolate" is made from cocoa butter, sugar, and milk solids; it contains no brown chocolate liquor. Real white chocolate is virtually impossible to obtain. (Often hydrogenated coconut oil and sugar is marketed as white chocolate.) It is difficult to work with and is generally not used for baking.

"Milk chocolate" contains chocolate liquor, sugar, flavorings, dried milk, and cocoa butter. It is eaten as candy and is not suitable for baking, because it does not react to heat in predictable ways.

Read the labels of chocolate products carefully and buy the finest product available. Not only does inferior chocolate offend the palate, but it may not even work in a recipe. To test the quality of chocolate, first scrutinize it by eye (fine chocolate is very dark, shiny, and smooth); smell it (fine chocolate should have a subtle but pungent aroma); break off a piece (fine chocolate will snap cleanly and crisply and the inside will not reveal any white streaks or blotches); finally, melt the chocolate (fine chocolate will melt smoothly and will not become gritty or rubbery). The taste of fine chocolate needs no description, although fine chocolates can have many different characters from cheesy to fruity to developed. There should be no aftertastes or foreign flavors.

Store chocolate well sealed, in a cool, dry place—ideally between 60°F. and 75°F. Do not refrigerate or freeze. Do not subject to radical temperature variations while in storage. Improperly stored chocolate may "bloom"; that is, some of the cocoa butter may rise to the surface, causing white blotches or spots. This does not affect the taste, but it looks unpalatable and is an indication that you should be more careful with this precious foodstuff.

## • COCOA •

Cocoa is the solid brown part of the cocoa bean with the cocoa butter or fat removed. Cocoa powder for baking is sold unsweetened. Unlike baking chocolate, most brands are pure and of high quality. Again, the European brands, Dröste in particular, win out in terms of taste, but all brands will produce successful results.

Cocoa is processed with alkali to neutralize naturally occurring bitter acids, to make it dissolve more readily, and to make it more di-

gestible. Alkalized cocoa is often called "Dutched" because the process was invented by Coenraad J. van Houten, a Dutchman. Alkalized cocoa is of a darker color. I have noticed no difference between alkalized and nonalkalized cocoa in recipes when only a few tablespoons of cocoa are used.

Store cocoa well sealed, in a cool, dry place away from light and pungent foodstuffs—ideally between 60°F. and 75°F. with less than 50 percent relative humidity.

## • SUGAR •

### *Granulated Sugar*

Common white granulated sugar is sucrose, a disaccharide consisting of units of glucose and fructose. It is made from sugarcane or sugar beets and is usually 100 percent pure. White granulated sugar is available in several crystal sizes: coarse, regular, and extra-fine or superfine. Regular sugar is suitable for all recipes in this book, and the volume quantities specified are for regular sugar. If substituting coarse or extra-fine sugar, always weigh the amount. A volume measurement of coarse sugar will weigh considerably less than an equal volume amount of regular sugar, and a volume amount of extra-fine sugar will weigh considerably more than an equal volume amount of regular sugar. Although the use of coarse sugar is not recommended, it may be substituted, but only in recipes where the sugar is melted, as in a genoise, buttercream, or custard.

Store sugar, well sealed, in a cool, dry place away from pungent foodstuffs.

### *Vanilla Sugar*

Vanilla sugar adds a depth of flavor to all baked goods. To make vanilla sugar, split a vanilla bean with a paring knife and place it in a

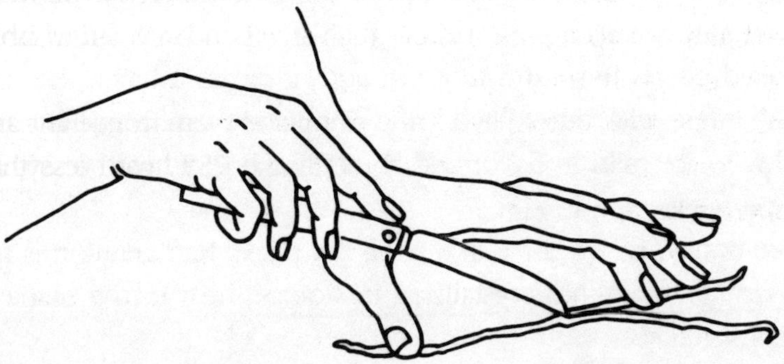

sealed container of granulated sugar. Allow it to steep for a few days or until the sugar smells like vanilla. A vanilla bean may be used and reused in this manner for about a year or until it is no longer aromatic. Vanilla sugar is infinitely superior to any extract, however purportedly pure. Use vanilla sugar in any recipe specifying sugar. In recipes also specifying a vanilla bean, reduce the amount by half if you are also using a pungent vanilla sugar.

### *Powdered or Confectioners' Sugar*

Powdered or confectioners' sugar is made from sugarcane or sugar beets, as is granulated sugar, but it is crushed and screened to produce its powdery texture. It generally has 3 percent cornflour to prevent caking. Powdered sugar should *always* be sifted before use. Store as you do granulated sugar.

## • HONEY •

Honey is a sweetener that is very different chemically from white sugar. No magic formula exists for substituting honey for sugar. Generally, one would use slightly less honey than sugar, adjusting the liquids in the recipe proportionally, but this method cannot always be relied upon. Honey retains more moisture than sugar and will aid in keeping baked goods fresh and moist. It adds a pleasant flavor, but can often interfere with other flavors and dominate them. Some honeys, like clover, are mild in flavor and some, like buckwheat honey, are more pungent.

Store honey, well sealed, in a cool, dry place. Refrigeration is not necessary. If honey has crystallized in storage, heat it to a manageable consistency.

## • EGGS •

Eggs are an essential ingredient in most cakes. Always buy the freshest eggs available. An egg that floats in water is not fresh. Eggs can be kept for several days unrefrigerated, but it is advisable to store even the freshest eggs in the refrigerator. The recipes in this book are based on U.S. Grade A large eggs, though volume measurements in cups are given as well. (I always have containers of yolks and whites left over in my refrigerator and appreciate volume measurements of eggs.) Eggs with brown shells are exactly the same inside as eggs with white shells. A thin shell that shatters rather than breaking cleanly indicates that the hens may have been fed hormones. Discard any eggs with cracked shells. If the salmonella bacteria is present it will grow in the cracked egg with no detectable signs or smells. It is easier to separate the whites from the yolks if the eggs are cold, but eggs beat more readily if they are at room temperature.

## • FLOUR •

Flour is made from grains such as wheat, rye, or rice and starchy (farinaceous) plants such as corn or potatoes. Flour is not necessarily a component of all cakes. (People with an intolerance or allergy to gluten will find several recipes for flourless cakes in this book.)

Wheat flour used for making cakes has the germ and the bran removed. Cake flour is made from "soft" summer wheat that has more starch than plain flour. Flour naturally bleaches itself with age, but sometimes cake flour is artificially bleached. Because cake flour is more starchy than plain flour, it tends to lump and must *always* be sifted before incorporation into a batter. Cake flour produces a lighter texture and finer crumb than plain flour. If plain flour is the only one available, mix it three parts to one part cornflour for recipes that specify cake flour.

Many factors interfere with an accurate measurement of flour by volume. Measuring flour strictly by weight is strongly recommended. However, if you do not wish to buy a scale, sift the flour and gently scoop it into the measuring utensil, being careful not to pack it down, and then level it with a knife.

The advent of self-raising flour was one step forward and two steps backward for baking. Not only did it condition the palate to accept foreign chemical tastes, it engendered the false impression that chemical leavening is necessary for baked goods to rise. With proper technique, any cake is "self-raising" without chemical additives. Self-raising flour contains added salt, baking soda, and baking powder. No recipe in this book calls for self-raising flour.

Always buy the freshest flour available and store it, well sealed, in a cool, dry place away from pungent foodstuffs.

## • BUTTER •

Most recipes in this book specify unsalted butter. You can find it in the freezer section of a grocery store and should store it in your own freezer, as unsalted butter turns sour more quickly than salted butter (salt acts as a preservative). Unsalted butter is sometimes called sweet butter, but this does not mean that sugar was added. (Fresh raw cream is slightly sweet, depending upon what the cows were fed.) Salted butter contains not only salt, but moisture, absorbed by the salt, both of which are foreign matters in cakes. Salted butter is more likely to contain coloring than unsalted butter. Using unsalted butter allows you to decrease the sugar that would otherwise be necessary to mask the incongruous salty taste. Measure whipped butter by the weight, not the volume measurements, as whipped butter weighs considerably less than an equal volume of unwhipped butter.

*Always* bring butter to a soft room temperature before incorporation into a batter or buttercream. If you are careless or rushed and attempt to use the butter before it is sufficiently soft, it will not be properly incorporated into the batter, glaze, or buttercream.

## • FLAVORINGS •

### *Vanilla Beans*

Vanilla beans are the seed pods of an orchid grown in the same geographic area as the cacao tree and are a beautiful shiny brown color. Vanilla and chocolate have been combined for thousands of years.

The Aztecs mixed vanilla and ground spices with cacao beans to make a frothy drink.

Vanilla beans are available in supermarkets, gourmet stores, and by mail order. They are between 4 and 8 inches long and can be fat and plump. Always look for the fattest, shiniest beans. Store vanilla beans directly in sugar. A vanilla bean should never be discarded until the smell has dissipated. As one bean can flavor many pounds of sugar, it is more economical to purchase a bean and reuse it than to use extract.

## *Flavor Extracts*

All alcohol-based flavor extracts—vanilla, almond, lemon, orange, brandy, or rum—leave an unacceptable bitter aftertaste reminiscent of the smell of tincture of iodine or paint thinner. Extracts are so grossly overused that many unsuspecting palates simply mistake what is common for what is natural. Compare the smell of a vanilla extract, however purportedly pure, to a real vanilla bean. Compare the smell of freshly blanched almonds to almond extract. Freshly grated citrus rinds smell better and are more pungent than any extract. Try to avoid all extracts and learn to prepare and appreciate natural flavors.

## *Spices*

Always use freshly ground whole spices. The flavor oils of preground spices dissipate quickly, leaving behind a residue of slightly flavorful powder. (See tips for grinding spices, page 52.) Store spices in a cool place out of the light. Exposure to light causes the flavor oils in spices to evaporate prematurely. An exposed spice shelf, far from being an ornamental touch to one's kitchen, is a monument to insipid eating. Store spices in a closed drawer or cupboard.

## *Coffee*

Coffee is a wonderful complement to the flavor of chocolate. For maximum taste use freshly roasted and ground coffee, brewed very strong.

## *Angelica*

Called the "Root of the Holy Ghost," angelica is a flavoring that has fallen out of common use in pastry making. It is available by mail order. Or, since it is a weed, very hardy and easy to grow, you might want to try growing your own. Angelica is slightly tart, but it is too distinct in flavor to be compared to anything else. Preserve the stalks in a sugar syrup made from one part sugar and one part water.

## *Nuts*

Nuts add a depth of flavor and a crunchy texture to cakes, and often can be used as the body of a cake instead of flour. Always buy fresh whole nuts and grind them yourself. Most health-food stores carry high-quality whole nuts. Never buy preground nuts, as nuts lose a lot of flavor once ground, and ground unblanched nuts may be mixed with nut skins left over from the blanching process by unscrupulous manufacturers. Store nuts in a cool, dry place or well sealed in the refrigerator. Nuts need not be frozen, and indeed the lipids (fats) in nuts undergo a chemical change once the nuts are frozen and may react in strange ways in some recipes. Always sample nuts before you buy. Do not buy nuts that are bitter and rubbery. Hazelnuts, particularly, if improperly stored become rubbery and resist grinding. Be especially cautious when buying nuts during the summer months. Nuts are usually harvested in autumn, and if improperly stored by wholesalers over the winter may go rancid or become rubbery or bitter. Measurement of nuts by weight is recommended. Nuts tightly packed into a measuring cup (hazelnuts in particular) will obviously weigh more than nuts loosely tossed into the vessel.

### *Fruits*

Always use high-quality fresh fruit. All the recipes in this book call for fresh fruit. If a particular fruit is not in season, do not substitute frozen or canned fruit but choose another recipe featuring dried fruit, or whatever fresh fruit is available. Homemade fruit jams, jellies, and marmalades are always tastier than their commercial counterparts. Jams can be made from dried fruits. Always rinse fruit. If you have any reason to believe that the fruit was grown with spray pesticides or treated with wax or coloring, soak the fruit for an hour in a saltwater solution (1 tablespoon salt per quart of water). Rinse thoroughly and rub dry. In the case of citrus fruits, white spots may appear after the fruit has soaked. This is undissolved wax. Try to rub it off.

Peel and slice fruit only immediately before using. Delicate fruit flavors are elusive and are eroded upon exposure to air. For instance, kiwi fruit will be almost tasteless a few hours after peeling and slicing.

### *Liqueurs*

Liqueur can complement the taste of chocolate by cutting the sweetness and adding a sophisticated, enhanced flavor. Use only the best liqueurs. They do represent a sizable investment, but if you compare the price of so-called flavor extracts, ounce per ounce, to the finest liqueur, you will discover the difference is negligible, considering the quality.

Many recipes in this book call for liqueurs as an optional ingredient. Children (and some adults) often do not care for the taste a liqueur imparts to a cake.

Store liqueurs, well sealed, out of the light.

## • CHEMICAL LEAVENING •

Chemical leavening agents such as baking powder, baking soda, and self-raising flour are not used in this book, with the exception of the recipe for Devil's Food Cake. Chemical leavening not only produces a wretched smell while a cake is baking, but necessitates an overabundance of sugar to mask the foreign chemical taste. Baking soda more properly belongs in an open box in the refrigerator to absorb odors, than in cakes.

## • SUBSTITUTIONS •

Certain nuts can be substituted for one another, depending on the fat content: walnuts and pecans; almonds, hazelnuts, and pine nuts; Brazil nuts and macadamias.

The grated rind of any citrus fruit can be substituted for that of any other citrus fruit, but remember that lime and grapefruit will be more tart and bitter than lemon and orange.

Certain liqueurs and liquors may be substituted for one another: brandy and cognac; whiskey, bourbon, Drambuie, and rum; Grand Marnier and Cointreau; liqueur kirsch and clear fruit brandy.

# TOOLS AND EQUIPMENT

## • MEASURING EQUIPMENT •

### *Scales*

There are two kinds of scales: balance and spring scales. On a balance scale, the weight of the ingredients exactly equals the calibrated weight on the other side of the fulcrum. Spring scales register weight

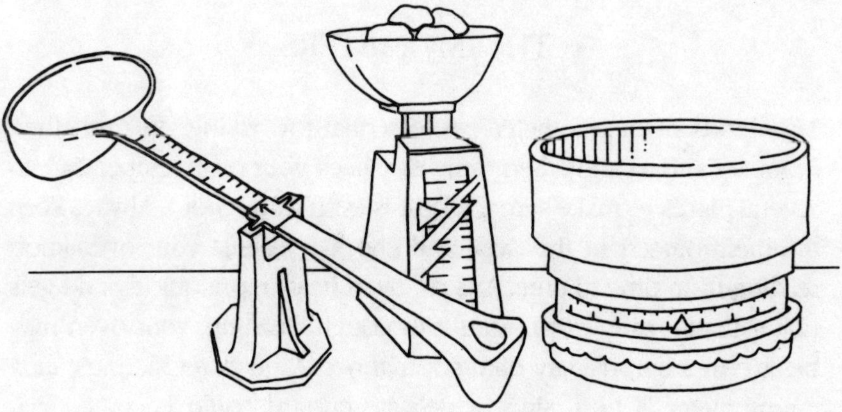

by means of tensile springs calibrated to a range of weights. Spring scales lose accuracy with age, as the springs tend to relax and stick. Test the accuracy of scales by placing a calculated weight on them, such as a pound of butter.

### *Volume Measures*

Volume measures are available in several materials: glass, metal, or plastic. Use glass or stainless steel. Aluminum reacts with certain acidic foodstuffs. Plastic may contaminate any warm or hot foodstuffs and can absorb odors from other foods, thus contaminating the ingredient being measured. Bent or dented cup measures do not measure accurately.

### *Measuring Spoons*

Measuring spoons are available in plastic or metal. Use stainless steel. Avoid plastic and aluminum for the reasons given above. Bent or dented spoons do not measure accurately.

## • THERMOMETERS •

Two kinds of thermometers are essential for baking: an oven thermometer and a candy thermometer. Check your oven temperature in several places to make sure the heat is even throughout. Always keep the thermometer in the oven and check it against your oven-knob reading from time to time. A clean oven heats more quickly and gets hotter than a dirty oven. After a thorough cleaning, your oven may behave in a surprisingly different manner. A quick-registering candy thermometer is best, since a delicate custard could become overcooked in the time it takes a slow-registering thermometer to report the temperature. Never insert a cold thermometer into a hot mixture; this could cause the glass encasement to shatter. On a cold day, warm the thermometer in tepid water.

## • SPOONS AND CHOPSTICKS •

The simple wooden spoon and the humble chopstick are essential stirring tools in every kitchen. Unlike metal, wood does not conduct heat. Do not allow wood splinters to split off into the food. Never use aluminum spoons. Stainless steel or ceramic is acceptable. Use a chopstick for procedures when the goal is to blend but not incorporate air into the mixture.

## • SPATULAS •

A flexible rubber spatula is an excellent tool for folding ingredients into a batter and scraping batter from the sides of a mixing bowl. Spatulas are available with wood and plastic handles. Palette knives are sometimes mistakenly referred to as spatulas. Choose whatever size spatula feels comfortable in your hand.

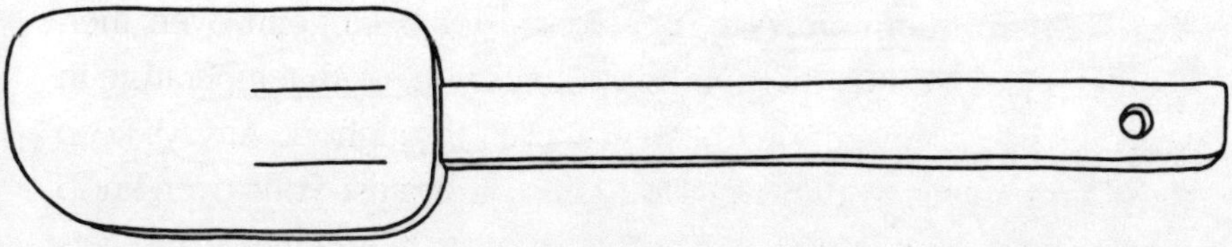

## • SCRAPERS •

A scraper is a firm but flexible thin piece of rubber, plastic, or metal with squared or rounded edges. To fold ingredients into a batter use a plastic or rubber scraper. Flour companies give rubber scrapers away to their bakery customers. A metal scraper is useful for making Chocolate Cigarettes (page 70) and for scraping batter or dough off a work surface.

## • KNIVES •

Several kinds of knives are essential to baking operations: a paring knife, a serrated knife, a chopping or "chef's" knife or cleaver, a palette knife, and an elbow-palette knife. Use a paring knife for paring and slicing fruits. Split a cake with a serrated knife. Chop chocolate with a chopping or "chef's" knife or cleaver. Palette knives are useful for spreading batter and decorating cakes. Elbow-palette knives are very efficient for decorating large cakes, spreading batter, and removing cakes stubbornly stuck to their pans.

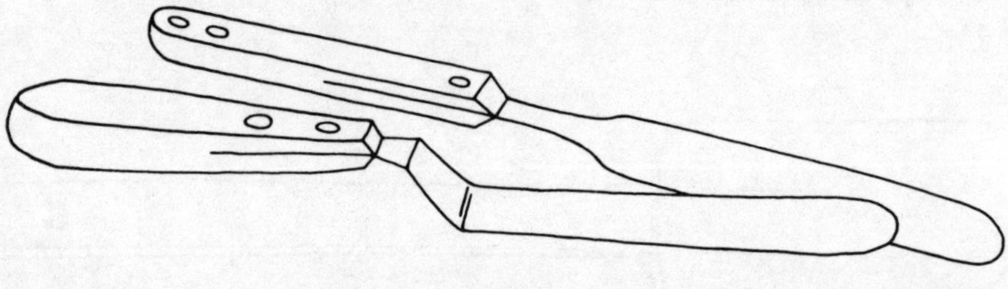

## • SCISSORS •

Scissors are essential in every kitchen. Specific baking operations for scissors include cutting a thin sheet cake into several layers (Doboshtorte) and cutting citrus rinds. Cheap, dull "kiddie" scissors are acceptable. Pinking shears will make an attractive edge for citrus rind.

## • GRATERS •

A hand grater is useful when a small amount of citrus rind is specified in a recipe. To grate a large amount, peel off the rind with a potato peeler, then use a food processor with the metal knife attachment.

## • POTATO PEELER •

A potato peeler comes in handy for peeling lemons or pears, and can be used to make Chocolate Curls, page 69.

## • PEAR CORER •

A pear corer cores not only pears but also apples and can be used to make Chocolate Curls, page 69.

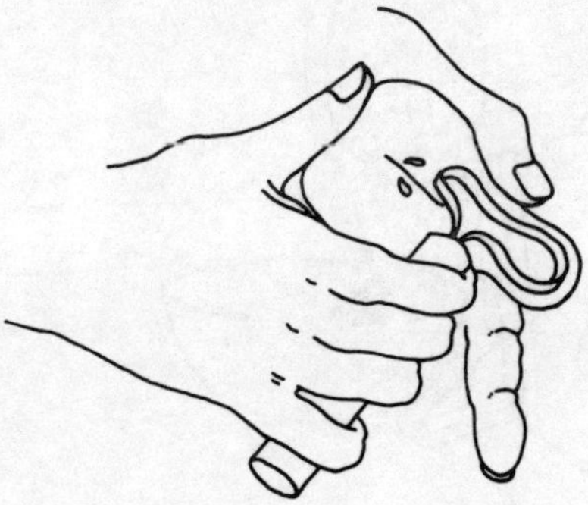

## • CHOPPING BLOCK •

Have separate chopping blocks for pastry, vegetable, and meat preparation. Hardwood is the best material, but special plastic boards available in cookware stores make good substitutes. Clean a chopping block with bleach occasionally to kill any bacteria lurking in the crevices.

## • HAND-OPERATED NUT • • AND CHOCOLATE GRINDERS •

Several brands, styles, and sizes of hand-operated nut and chocolate grinders are available. The texture of hand-ground nuts and chocolate is different from that produced by powerful machines; it is drier and more flaky. Hand grinders also have the advantage that any nutshells that may remain after the nuts are supposedly shelled will clog and stop a hand grinder and may then be removed.

## • ELECTRIC BLENDERS •

Electric blenders are useful for making crumbs from stale cake and grinding nuts. Always sift nuts ground in a blender, as the particles may not be of uniform size. Grind only a small portion at a time and take care not to turn the nuts into nut butter.

## • FOOD PROCESSORS •

Food processors with the metal blade may be used to grind nuts and chocolate and to make crumbs from stale cake. Place the chocolate or nuts and the blade in the freezer for a few minutes before grinding (do not completely freeze); the chocolate or nuts will be brittle and will not turn into paste when processed; a little sugar or flour added to the nuts also helps (subtract it from the amount specified in the recipe). A food processor can also chop dried fruit; add a little flour or sugar to dried fruit to keep it dry. Peel lemon rinds and then grate them with a little sugar in the food processor. Slice fruit for making jam or marmalade in the food processor, but do not slice fruit used as a garnish, such as poached pears or kiwi fruit. Blend plain flour and cornflour in the food processor for simulated cake flour (see page 13). Flour, cornflour, and powdered sugar can be "sifted" quickly by "processing" them for 5 seconds.

## • SIFTERS AND STRAINERS •

Several kinds of sifters are available, including the hand-squeezed type and electric models. A wire-mesh basket can double as a sifter and a strainer. Wire-mesh strainers are available with plastic and metal mesh. Do not use the plastic variety for straining hot substances. A food processor can be used to "sift" flour, as mentioned above.

## • MIXING BOWLS •

Mixing bowls are available in many materials: ceramic, glass, enamel, stainless steel, copper, and plastic. Copper does indeed react magically with beaten egg whites, but a copper bowl is not a necessity. Avoid plastic bowls—they may absorb odors and grease and make beating egg whites impossible. Bowls with snap-on lids are handy for storing leftovers.

## • WHIPPING TOOLS •

### *Whisks*

Whisks are indispensable tools for many baking operations, including beating eggs, cooking custards, making buttercreams, and creaming butter. Use whatever size and weight whisk feels comfortable in your hand. Whisks are available with wire and wooden handles; the wooden-handled variety is preferable, because wood does not absorb heat. Make sure that the whisk is grease-free before beating egg whites.

### *Hand-Operated Eggbeaters*

Eggbeaters are marvelously efficient tools but are not interchangeable with whisks. Use them for beating eggs, egg whites, or cream, but not for cooking custards and beating butter into buttercream; too much air will be incorporated.

### *Hand-Held Electric Mixers*

If you take satisfaction from hand beating, by all means do not deny yourself the experience. However, hand beating until one is blue in the face does not make a good cook or baker; electric mixers accomplish the same beating action as manually operated mixers and whisks. If you find the boredom and noise of a hand-held electric mixer annoying, be ingenious and rig up some system whereby the mixer is supported in the mixing bowl. Hand-held electric mixers are frequently discarded because of new developments in food preparation appliances; almost any junk or secondhand store has many electric mixers for a few dollars.

### *Electric Mixers*

An electric mixer is a wonderful convenience for baking. Most brands are solidly made and will last a lifetime. If possible, buy an electric mixer with several attachments: a whisk head, a pastry paddle, and a dough hook. A tapered mixing bowl is more efficient for beating eggs, but a rounded bowl is adequate. Most electric mixers do not turn themselves off automatically when overheated. Place your hand on the motor housing occasionally when lengthy beating operations are required to make certain the machine does not overheat. If the motor becomes too hot, turn the mixer off until completely cooled. Have two bowls for the electric mixer if possible; many cakes require separate operations for beating egg whites and egg yolks.

## • COOKING UTENSILS •

### *Double Boiler*

A double boiler, or bain-marie, is essential for working with chocolate. A heavy mixing bowl placed over a pan of water can serve the same function. If the bowl is smaller in diameter than the pan, make a foil collar to keep the steam away from the melting or cooking mixture. Check occasionally to see that the bottom of the double boiler does indeed have water in it; steam can escape even though the top fits snugly into the bottom of the double boiler.

### *Saucepans and Stockpots*

Saucepans and stockpots are available in a variety of materials. Enameled cast iron and stainless steel are good choices, as they are completely inert and safe with all foodstuffs. Copper is an efficient heat conductor, but copper, and the tin with which copper pots are often lined, does react with certain foodstuffs if they are stored in it. To be safe, never store any food in a copper vessel. Avoid aluminum, as it reacts with certain acidic foodstuffs leaving a bitter metallic taste.

## • ROLLING PINS •

Two kinds of rolling pins are available: the simple dowel type, some with slightly tapered ends, and the type with a handle and metal rod and ball bearings. The simple dowel type allows greater sensitivity to the dough and is preferred by the professional baker. Using a dowel-type rolling pin requires more skill, but it is a skill worth cultivating. Never submerge a rolling pin with a metal shaft in water; the metal will rust.

## • PAPER PRODUCTS •

### *Parchment Paper*

Parchment paper is used to line the bottoms of cake pans and baking sheets. It is treated with silicon and is available in many cooking equipment stores in precut round sizes and sheets. Parchment is head and shoulders above wax paper, but it is expensive when purchased in small quantities. Bread dough does not stick to unbuttered parchment, but the paper must be buttered and floured for cake batters.

### *Wax Paper*

Wax paper can be used to line cake pans and baking sheets and to wrap cakes for storage. However, when baking at a temperature over 375°F. the wax begins to burn and smells horrible. To cut a wax paper cake pan liner, place the baking pan upside down on top of the wax paper and trace around it with a sharp knife; gently tear away the excess paper; or cut the paper with scissors.

### *Cardboard Cake Supports*

Corrugated cardboard cake supports are available precut in some cooking-supply stores, or you can cut them out of corrugated cardboard yourself; cut several at a time. Large or very dense or moist cakes can be inverted directly onto a cardboard support that has been sprinkled with sugar to lessen the chance of cracking the cake when transferring it from cooling rack to serving platter. Cakes to be frozen should be supported by a piece of cardboard lest their shape be deformed if pushed against less malleable objects.

### *Doilies*

For that professional look, filigree-patterned doilies set off a cake dramatically and are available in an almost infinite variety in supermarkets and other stores. If you place a cake on a doily before decorating, be careful not to get any decorating material on the doily; place strips of wax paper over the doily to keep it clean.

## • PLASTIC WRAP AND PLASTIC BAGS •

Plastic wrap and plastic bags are useful for storing undecorated cakes. Allow cakes to cool thoroughly before placing in contact with plastic.

## • BAKEWARE •

Baking pans and sheets are of several materials: tin, aluminum, glass, and ceramic. Each material has different heat-conducting properties that will affect baking times. Aluminum is an acceptable material for a baking sheet, but never bake directly on it, as aluminum can affect the taste of food; cover the surface with wax or parchment paper. The recipes in this book were tested with tin baking pans and sheets (see Mail Order Guide, page 229, for sources of good baking pans). The baking times for cakes in pans of another material may vary. Use your own judgment and follow the guidelines for determining when a cake is done (page 53).

Always purchase the sturdiest, heaviest-gauge baking pans and sheets available. Inspect to make sure no scratches or dents mar the surface. Metal pans may improve or "temper" with age; metal pans from bakery surplus sales and flea markets may be better than newly manufactured metalware. "Bake" and cool a new pan by itself several times before using or a batter may stick. Dry non–stainless steel baking pans thoroughly or they may rust.

### *Baking Sheets*

Have at least two 12-by-18-inch baking sheets with side rims. They are the same thing as jelly-roll pans, but not the same as a cookie sheet.

### *Baking Pans*

Baking pans come in an infinite variety of shapes: round, square, rectangular, loaf, fluted or brioche, heart- and animal-molded shapes. Springform pans, or pans with removable bottoms, are also available.

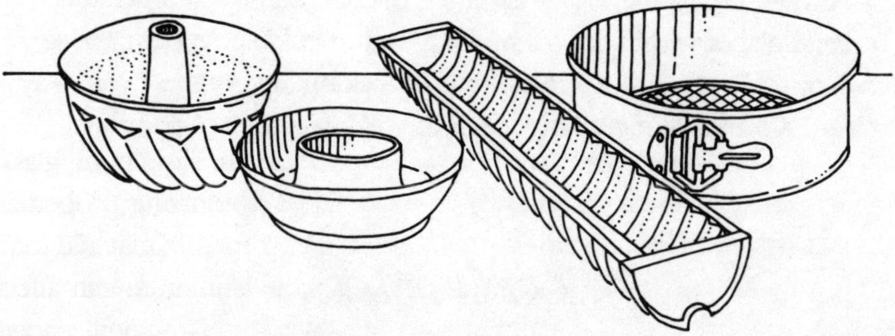

### *Baking Pans with Center Holes*

Baking pans with center holes, sometimes called tube pans, expose more of the batter to direct heat. When a tube pan is specified in a recipe, do not substitute another kind of pan merely with the same liquid capacity; divide the batter into two pans, thus exposing more of the batter to the surface. Some tube pans, such as a Savarin pan, have a wide center hole, and some, such as an angel food cake pan, have a narrow center hole. Kugelhopf and Bundt pans are patterned on the sides and have narrow center holes.

## • OVEN •

An oven is the essential piece of baking equipment. Several kinds exist for household use: gas or electric, convection, and microwave. The recipes in this book were tested with a regular gas home oven.

Cakes baked in a convection oven will require less baking time. Professional bakeries have used convection ovens for years and several brands of convection ovens are now available for home use (but most brands are not insulated properly). A microwave oven is not suitable for baking. Melting chocolate in a microwave oven is not recommended, as it sometimes turns into a rubbery mess.

Always keep a thermometer in the oven; check the temperature in several places within the oven. If any hot or cold spots exist, rotate a baking cake to assure uniformity of baking. Keep the oven very clean. A buildup of cooking residues will affect the temperature.

## • COOLING RACKS •

Cakes should be inverted onto racks to cool. Racks allow steam from the baked cake to evaporate; cakes cooled in the pan can become soggy, and if the butter on the pan has hardened the cake may stick. Choose sturdy racks with thin crossbars fairly close together, about ½ inch apart. An oven rack can double as a cooling rack if the crossbars are thin and close together.

## • DECORATING EQUIPMENT •

### *Palette Knives*

The proper name for the tool used to decorate a cake is a palette knife, although it is sometimes mistakenly referred to as a spatula. Choose a flexible palette knife of high-quality stainless steel. Palette knives are available with plastic, metal, or wooden handles and in several sizes. Choose whatever feels comfortable and balanced in your hand. Having several sizes of palette knives is recommended, since it is easier to decorate a small cake with a small knife and a large cake with a larger knife.

## *Pastry Bags*

Pastry bags, also called forcing or piping bags, are available in a variety of sizes and materials: nylon, plastic, or canvas with plastic or rubber coating, or you can make one with parchment paper or wax paper. Lightweight nylon, the material preferred by professionals, is the most sensitive and easy to control. Have at least two pastry bags, one large (18 inches) and one small (12 inches). Refilling a pastry bag is a messy operation; for big jobs it is better to have a large one and fill it only once. However, pastry bags can be unwieldy when only a small amount of filling is called for.

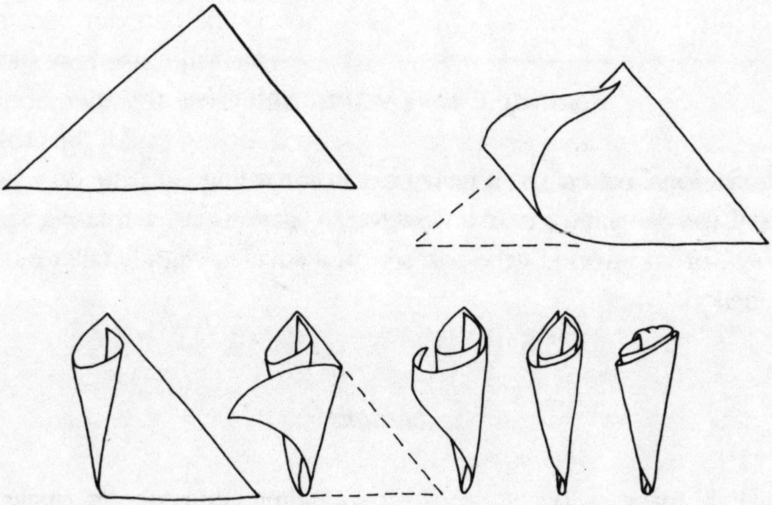

## *Pastry Bag Tips*

Pastry bag tips or nozzles are available in a myriad of sizes and shapes. Only a few are necessary for classical decoration: plain nozzles, ¼-, ½-, and 1-inch sizes, a rosette or star tip, a writing tip, and a ruffle border.

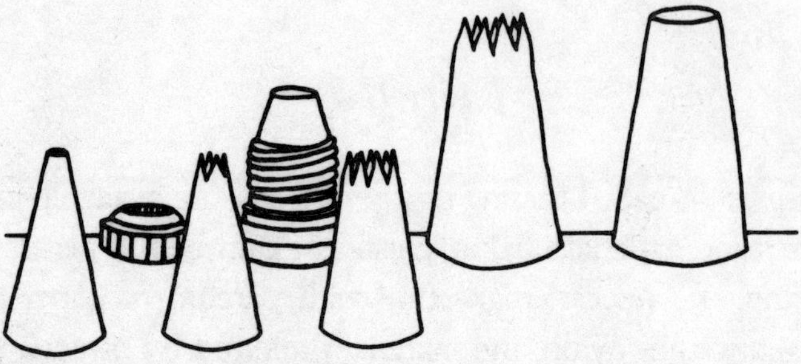

*Texturing Equipment*

Special decorating "combs" are available to texture buttercream, whipped cream, or glaze, or you can simply use a *clean* hair comb or fork.

*Rotating Cake Decorating Pedestal*

Professional bakers use a heavy cast-iron rotating flat plate on a pedestal for decorating cakes. However, a lazy Susan, a rotating spice shelf, or an inverted cake pan set on a smaller, slightly taller pan is functional.

*Stencils*

A doily makes a lovely stencil for sprinkling confectioners' sugar or cocoa onto cakes. To make your own stencil, cut a piece of paper the size of the cake, fold it in half, quarters, eighths, sixteenths, and so forth, and clip away segments with scissors (the way children make paper "snowflakes"). Any household object, such as an unusual slotted spoon, can be used as a stencil.

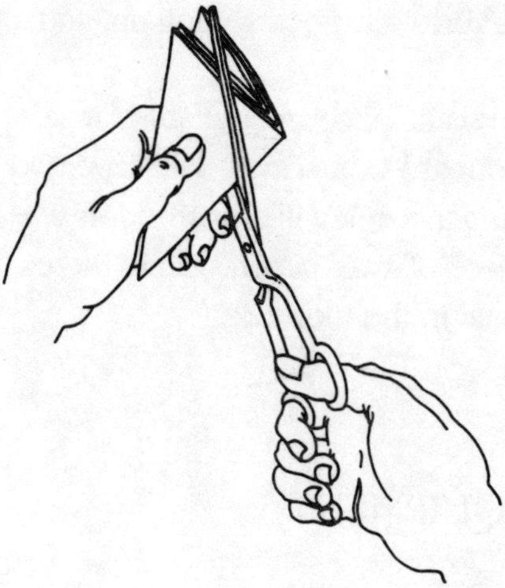

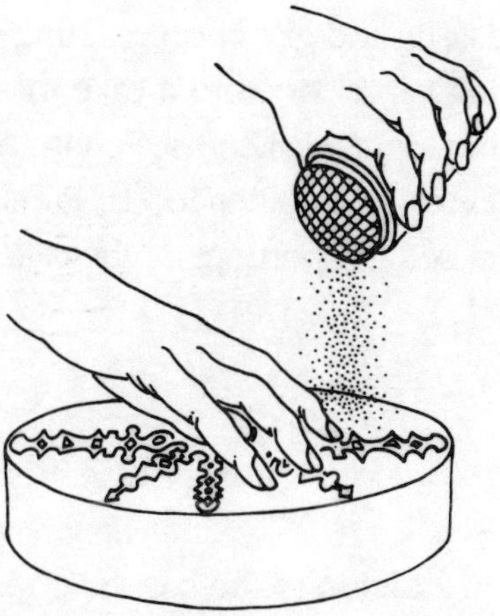

*Sugar Shakers*

Large cylindrical shakers are available to sprinkle sugar, or use a salt shaker with large holes.

## • SERVING EQUIPMENT •

*Pedestaled Cake Plate*

Cake plates are often elevated for dramatic presentation. Pedestaled cake plates are available in porcelain, cut glass, silver, pewter, and other materials, and are often beautifully ornate. Cutting a cake on a curved-rim plate is awkward; serve cake on a flat plate if possible.

*Cake Servers*

Cut a cake with a very sharp knife, plain-edged or serrated. Any broad, flat, thin utensil can be used to serve cake.

## • STORAGE •

Plastic and glass domes fitting onto a cake plate are available for storing cakes, or store a cake in a cardboard box sealed with tape. Do not store a cake unsealed in the refrigerator; it will absorb odors and tastes from other foods. Press a piece of wax paper against the exposed cut portions of the cake to seal in the moisture.

## • CLEANUP EQUIPMENT •

In addition to the basic sponges, rags, and scouring pads, a plastic or metal scraper is useful. Utensils soiled by chocolate must be washed with soap and hot water to dissolve the fats in the chocolate.

# PROFESSIONAL TIPS AND SECRETS

## • CLEAN UTENSILS •

Maintain impeccably clean utensils. Egg whites are affected by the slightest amount of grease. Chocolate spills are better cleaned as they occur. Have a garbage bag close at hand. Excess flour is better scraped off the work surface with a rubber or metal scraper than by wetting it with a sponge.

## • USING WAX PAPER •

To facilitate cleanup, sift flour, grind nuts, grate chocolate, and pulverize spices onto wax paper instead of using bowls that must be washed. Beat egg whites first, if you have only one bowl, and transfer them onto a piece of wax paper. Egg yolks may be beaten in the same bowl as the egg whites without washing it, but the reverse is not true.

## • BUTTERING PANS •

Grease a pan with *butter*, preferably unsalted, not margarine, shortening, oil, or any other substitute. The butter should be very soft or melted. Use your hands or a piece of paper, or reserve a special pastry brush to butter pans. Coat the pans thoroughly but lightly with the butter. For pans with flat bottoms, cut a piece of wax paper the size of the pan and press it into the buttered bottom; make sure there are no air pockets. Butter the top of the paper or turn it over so the side that was pressed against the buttered pan is up. (Turning the paper over saves the step of buttering the paper twice.) Lightly dust the pan with flour or sugar. If the oven has any hot spots, do not use sugar, which may melt or caramelize, causing the cake to stick.

## • WORKING WITH EGGS •

### *Separating*

Before separating an egg, have two bowls or cups ready. No fancy gizmo works as well as separating eggs by hand. Sharply rap the egg against a blunt edge to break it approximately in half across the width.

METHOD I: Transfer the yolk from one half of the shell to the other half while liberating the whites into a container. Place the egg yolks in a separate container.

METHOD II: Place the whole egg in your hand and allow the whites to drip through your fingers into a bowl or cup while keeping the yolk intact. Transfer the yolk to another bowl.

Eggs are easier to separate when cold, but allow them to warm up a bit before beating. Always separate eggs cleanly; do not allow any bits of the yolks to contaminate the whites (a little of the whites sticking to the yolks is acceptable, however).

## *Beating Egg Whites*

Air beaten into egg whites, with or without the addition of sugar, is the basic leavening agent of most of the cakes in this book. Egg whites beat more readily if they are at room temperature. They will attain full volume even if they are cold, but the beating takes much longer. Myths abound regarding beating egg whites. Some recipe books insist that using a copper bowl is the only way to properly beat egg whites, or that a pinch of salt, cream of tartar, arrowroot, or a combination thereof is mandatory for stabilizing or achieving full volume in beating egg whites. I have never found any of these additives necessary for either achieving volume or stabilizing egg whites. Perhaps there are other factors involved and at certain longitudes, latitudes, elevations, barometric pressures, humidities, or positions of the stars, a pinch of something would be advisable. Experiment with and without additives to beat egg whites. If you need, or think you need, an additive in your particular locale or clime, use your own judgment. In my experience, the only rule never to violate regarding beating egg whites is that the whipping tool and bowl be absolutely fat-free.

Egg whites beaten with no sugar will not peak as firmly as those beaten with sugar; when lightly touched, the egg whites will mound into a little hill-like shape, but will not actually form peaks. Beat sugarless egg whites until stiff but not dry.

Egg whites beaten with sugar become very shiny and will peak. For most cakes in this book, the egg whites should be beaten until the peaks keep their shape but fall over into a hook. Egg whites beaten with sugar for a meringue should be beaten until the peaks are even stiffer and do not fall over into a hook. Do not allow beaten egg whites to sit around more than 5 to 10 minutes before incorporating them into a batter. Because most of the following recipes call for beating the egg whites first, you must learn to work efficiently in order to add the other ingredients before the whites have fallen. It is sometimes possible to beat them again, however.

*Beating Egg Yolks*

As with egg whites, air can be beaten into egg yolks for leavening purposes. Egg yolks have a creamy consistency and are pale yellow in color when thoroughly beaten. Thoroughly beaten egg yolks will fall in ribbons from the beating utensil.

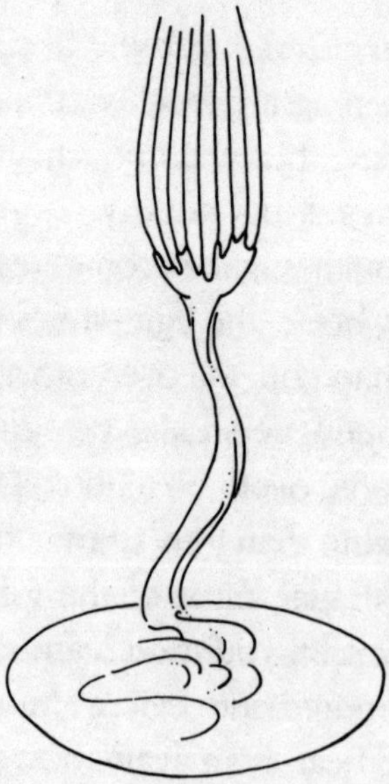

## *Beating Whole Eggs*

Beating the whole egg with sugar is the basis for the genoise family of cakes. To achieve maximum volume heat the egg-sugar mixture in the top of a double boiler, over hot, but not boiling, water, while whisking. The mixture should reach 125°F., and the whisk marks

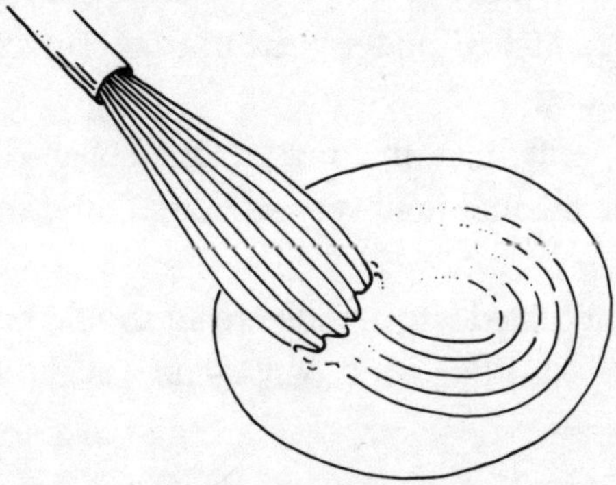

keep their shape. If yellow flecks appear, the mixture has been scorched and the eggs will be scrambled; throw it out and start over.

## *Folding Ingredients into Beaten Eggs and Folding in Egg Whites*

Mastering the technique of folding other ingredients into beaten eggs is essential to producing light, even-textured cakes. The goal is to homogenize all the ingredients while minimizing the release of air beaten into the eggs. Sprinkle the dry ingredients, about one-third at a time, into the beaten eggs or egg whites; then with a broad flat tool, such as a rubber spatula, scraper, or with your bare hands, reach to the bottom of the mixing bowl and bring the bottom batter up through the rest of the batter while scraping the sides of the bowl. Repeat this procedure turning the bowl as you do so only until all the ingredients are homogenized; *do not overmix*. Be gentle, but quick and efficient.

## • WORKING WITH BUTTER •

Butter can act like a number of different substances depending upon its temperature. Butter must always be brought to room temperature and be of a soft consistency before being incorporated into the mixture. *Do not be cavalier regarding butter temperatures.*

Melt butter over low heat or in a preheating oven. Do not allow the butter to brown. Melted butter need not be clarified for any of the recipes in this book.

Some recipes specify that the butter and sugar or honey be "creamed"; beat the mixture until very smooth, fluffy, and no longer gritty.

Butter to be incorporated into a buttercream should be so warm as to be almost soupy and the same consistency as the custard into which it is beaten.

## • WORKING WITH CHOCOLATE •

### *Measuring*

Always measure chocolate by weight. Chocolate is often sold in 1-ounce squares. "Mini" chocolate chips will pack tighter into a volume measure than will "regular" chocolate chips, which in turn will be different in weight per unit volume from chopped, grated, or shaved chocolate. Hand-grated chocolate sometimes is affected by static electricity, making it impossible to measure by volume.

### *Grinding or Grating*

Chocolate can be ground or grated in a number of ways: with a vegetable grater, nut grater, or food processor with the metal blade. An electric blender is unsuitable for grating chocolate—the action of the blender generates too much heat, causing the chocolate to melt immediately. If using a food processor, put the chocolate to be ground and the blade into the freezer for a few minutes before grinding. *Be careful not to allow the chocolate to freeze.* Simply let it become brittle.

## *Melting Chocolate*

Melting is a critical operation when working with chocolate. The cocoa butter in chocolate is a complex of many different lipid compounds (fats) each with a different melting temperature. First, grate or chop the chocolate into very small pieces. Place it in the top of a double boiler filled with warm water. To be safe, never let the water get above 140°F. and never let the chocolate itself get hotter than 100°F. Note that this is much lower than boiling (212°F) or even simmering water. Never melt chocolate over direct heat. Be warned that chocolate melted in a microwave oven sometimes turns rubbery and must be thrown out. Remember that like a watched pot, watched chocolate never melts; do not be heedless or impatient by trying to melt chocolate too quickly over too high a heat. Stir chocolate with a wooden spoon or chopstick while it is melting to equally distribute the heat, but make sure your stirring tool is very dry. If your melted chocolate seems rubbery or gluelike: (1) It simply may be inferior chocolate treated with stabilizers and emulsifiers that break down when exposed to heat. (2) It may have been contaminated by steam escaping from the bottom of the double boiler. (Ironically, the addition of a little *more* water—1 teaspoon—can sometimes cause the chocolate to become smooth again. If that is not successful, try a little butter. (Unsweetened and coating chocolate are especially prone to being contaminated by water.) (3) It was melted at too high a temperature. Perhaps rubbery chocolate can be incorporated into a batter, but never into a buttercream or glaze.

### *Cooling Melted Chocolate*

Cooling or "tempering" melted chocolate is another critical operation. Tempering stabilizes the fats in chocolate, which is important if it is to have the correct texture. Tempering is not necessary for chocolate that is to be incorporated into a batter because it will be subjected to more heat again in the oven, but for a beautiful, shiny chocolate glaze or buttercream, take heed. Change the water in the bottom of the double boiler from warm to cool or remove the top of the double boiler and let the chocolate cool at room temperature. (Cover the bottom of the double boiler so the steam does not condense on the chocolate.) Since glaze and buttercream have additional cream and/or butter, you need not cool the chocolate completely and then raise the temperature again as confectioners must do. Glaze should be slightly cooler than body temperature (94°F.) or cool enough to set up on a cake. If the glaze is too hot some of it will be absorbed into the cake and the rest will run off. Glaze that is too cool will not pour properly. Buttercream may require refrigeration before it is the proper temperature for spreading. Sometimes chocolate glaze crystallizes after it has cooled. This can be prevented by adding a little (½ teaspoon) corn syrup, honey, glucose, or any other sugar other than the white sugar in chocolate. The two different sugar molecules prevent the crystallization process.

## • WORKING WITH FLOUR, CORNFLOUR, • • AND COCOA •

Many factors interfere with accurate measurement of a dry ingredient by volume: humidity, the fineness to which it was ground, and the method of placing it into measurers. If you do not have a scale, sift the dry ingredient and then gently scoop it into the measurer, being careful not to pack it down, and then level it off with a knife.

Dry ingredients must always be sifted before incorporation into a batter. Sift onto a piece of wax paper to facilitate cleanup.

## • WORKING WITH NUTS •

### *Blanching*

Nuts are blanched to remove the skins, added salt, or both. Blanched nuts have a more delicate taste and finer texture than unblanched nuts. To blanch nuts, cover them with boiling water. Allow the nuts to steep in the water for about 10 minutes. (Do not discard the nut water; use it to make bread or add it to stock.) Squeeze the nut skins off between your thumb and your forefinger. Pat dry. (Do not discard the nut skins, but toast and add to bread, rice, or cereal.) Whole almonds with their skins can always be blanched. Walnuts and pecans need not be blanched. Pine nuts and macadamia nuts are usually sold without the skins but should be blanched if any salt has been added. Hazelnuts should be roasted and then their skins rubbed off. Dry blanched nuts thoroughly if they are to be stored; mold will grow quickly on damp nuts.

### *Roasting*

Roasting nuts develops the flavors and makes for a crunchier texture. To roast nuts, place them on a baking sheet and put under the broiler until the nuts make "popping" and cracking noises, become slightly brown in color, and exude a nutty odor. Shake the baking sheet occasionally to equally distribute the nuts. Nuts on the sides of the baking sheet may roast more quickly and become burned in the time it takes the rest of the nuts to roast. Rotate the baking sheet if your oven has any hot spots. Burned nuts taste and smell wretched and must be discarded. If the nuts have been improperly stored and have absorbed moisture, roast briefly.

### *Sliced Nuts*

Sliced nuts can be an attractive garnish. Slicing nuts by hand is not recommended; buy packaged sliced nuts.

## *Chopped Nuts*

Chopped nuts are used as a garnish or as a component of batters. Chop nuts with a "chopping" or "chef's" knife or a cleaver. A blender or food processor grinds nuts too finely for them to be considered "chopped." With a rolling pin, crush nuts in a plastic bag or between two pieces of wax paper for approximately the same effect.

## *Grinding Nuts*

Nuts ground to a meal (*mehl* is the German word for flour) can be used in place of wheat flour, adding a wonderful flavor and crunchy texture to a cake. Also, cakes made with nuts instead of flour will stay fresh longer. Make sure the nuts are very dry before grinding; improperly stored nuts, which may have absorbed moisture, should be lightly roasted before grinding. Nuts can be ground in a hand-operated grinder, in an electric blender, or in a food processor. To prevent nuts from becoming a mushy nut butter while being ground in powerful electric equipment, lightly coat them with sugar or flour. (Subtract this sugar or flour from the amount specified in the recipe.)

## *Sifting Nuts*

Sift ground nuts through a wire mesh strainer to remove any large pieces. Sifting may not be necessary if the nuts were ground in a food processor, but it is usually necessary if an electric blender was used.

## *Substituting Cake Crumbs for Nuts*

Up to half the finely ground nuts by weight (not volume) in a recipe can be replaced with cake crumbs.

## • WORKING WITH SUGAR •

### *Measuring*

If granulated sugar has not absorbed any moisture it can usually be accurately measured in volume units: 1 cup equals 8 ounces. However, powdered or confectioners' sugar must be weighed for an exact measurement. If you do not have a scale, sift the confectioners' sugar, gently scoop it into a measurer, being careful not to pack it down, and level it off with a knife.

## • WORKING WITH FRUIT •

### *Fresh Fruit*

When using fresh fruit, do not pare and slice until the last minute. Fresh fruit flavors are elusive and dissipate upon exposure to the air. Allow excessively juicy fruit to drain on towels before using as a garnish, or the juice may bleed into the buttercream, glaze, or whipped cream and look very messy.

### *Blanching Fruit*

If dried fruit was treated with sulfur or contains preservatives, blanch it by pouring boiling water over the fruit. Allow to steep for 1 minute and then drain off the water.

### *Chopping Dried Fruit*

Coat dried fruit with a little flour (subtract this flour from the amount specified in the recipe) to prevent the fruit from sticking together when chopped. Use a "chopping," or "chef's," knife, or cleaver to chop fruit by hand, or use a food processor with steel knife. Put only ¼ cup in the food processor at a time and turn it on and off quickly.

## • GRINDING WHOLE SPICES •

There are many ways to grind whole spices: in a mortar and pestle, with spice grinders or graters, in coffee grinders, or by smashing with a hammer. Use whatever method is convenient and achieves a powdery consistency. Large spices such as nutmeg or allspice may first have to be smashed with a hammer between two pieces of paper before grinding. A special tool exists for grating nutmeg and is called, appropriately enough, a nutmeg grater. Or, use the finest side of a cheese grater.

## • WORKING WITH VANILLA •

Reuse a vanilla bean to make vanilla sugar until the bean is very hard, dry, and no longer aromatic. Break the dry bean up into small segments and powder it in an electric blender or food processor. Add this vanilla powder to sugar to taste before adding to a batter.

## • MAKING CAKE CRUMBS •

Save the stale ends of cakes or entire unsuccessful cakes for recycling into cake crumbs. Break up the cake into small pieces and allow them to dry out in a warm place for a few days, or place in a 150°F.–200°F. oven for 15 minutes, or until very dry. Grind in an electric blender or food processor. Store, well sealed, at room temperature. Up to half the finely ground nuts in a recipe can be replaced by cake crumbs (by weight, not volume).

## • BAKING •

The oven door should not be opened during the first 15 minutes of baking. After this critical time, the oven door may be opened and closed very gradually; drastic changes in pressure could cause the cake to fall. Properly beaten cake batters are not overly sensitive "prima donnas." A delicate genoise batter once survived a 3.5 earthquake with the epicenter one mile from my oven.

### *Oven Circulation*

Air must be allowed to circulate freely around a baking cake to assure uniformity of baking. Always place the racks in the center of the oven. Allow at least 2 inches on every side of the pan or sheet. Do not attempt to fill more than two racks in the oven with baking sheets, or circulation will be impaired. Do not attempt to bake a cake simultaneously with any pungent or grease-spattering foodstuff.

### *How to Tell When Your Cake Is Done*

Several guidelines help in telling when a cake is done, although the exact degree of doneness is a matter of preference. The first indication that a cake may be fully baked is that a wonderful aroma emanates from the oven. As with most baked goods, when the liquids in the batter or dough are transformed into solids, steam, with the characteristic baked smell, is given off. A fully baked cake will seem set and dry on top and will sometimes shrink away from the sides of the pan. If you prefer a very moist, almost soufflé-like cake, a knife inserted into the center of the cake should not come out completely clean. Always invert these somewhat underbaked cakes onto cardboard. I find cakes baked in this manner rather indigestible; a better rule is that a knife inserted into the center of the cake should come out clean, that is, with no unbaked batter sticking to the knife.

## • COOLING A CAKE •

### *Racks*

After a cake has been out of the oven for 2 minutes, it should be inverted onto a cooling rack. Be very gentle in this operation; a little tapping of the pan is permissible, but a warm cake hit too forcefully may end up a pile of crumbs. Cooling on the rack allows the steam to escape instead of being trapped within the cake, which can make the cake soggy. If the cake has not shrunk away from the sides of the pan, loosen it by running a blunt knife around the edge before inverting.

### *Cardboard Cake Supports*

To prevent cracking and to facilitate transferring a cake from the cooling rack to the serving platter, invert large moist or dense cakes onto a piece of corrugated cardboard cut to the size of the cake and sprinkled with sugar to prevent the cake from sticking; then cool on a rack. Decorate and serve the cake directly on this support or slide the cake off the cardboard onto a serving platter with a wide, flat spatula. Cakes to be frozen should always be wrapped supported by a piece of cardboard, lest their shape be deformed if pushed against any less malleable objects.

### *Cooling Cakes Baked in Springform Pans*

If the cake has not shrunk away from the sides of the pan, run a blunt knife around the edge. Then loosen the springform and cool the cake for 10 minutes. Gently invert onto a rack or a cardboard support resting on a rack to finish the cooling.

### *How to Unstick Cakes*

If a cake has stuck because the pan surface was improperly prepared, there may be no hope of removing the cake intact. Try to budge a stuck cake with an elbow palette knife or with a flexible straight knife. If the cake has stuck to the pan because the coating butter has cooled to the hardening point, put the cake back in a warm oven for about 1 minute to liquefy the butter; then invert immediately.

### *Removing Wax or Parchment Paper*

Do not remove the wax or parchment paper if the cake is to be frozen; the paper will help preserve the freshness. If the cake is to be decorated immediately, remove the paper when the cake has cooled.

## • STORING UNDECORATED CAKES •

After a cake has completely cooled, it should be sealed off from air either by wrapping or with buttercream, glaze, or confectioners' sugar. Wrap a cake with plastic wrap, in plastic bags, foil, or wax paper, sealing with tape if necessary. Most cakes respond well to freezing if properly wrapped. Freezing is a more effective way of preserving freshness than refrigeration, but if the cake is to be decorated within 24 hours after being baked, refrigeration is sufficient.

## • PREPARING A CAKE FOR DECORATION •

If the cake has been frozen, thaw it in the refrigerator or at room temperature.

### *Splitting a Cake*

Do not completely thaw a cake if it is to be split into two or more layers. Put a freshly baked cake in the freezer for a few moments to facilitate splitting. To split a cake, take a sharp serrated knife, then firmly anchor your elbow against your body, your hipbone (I always thought my protruding hipbones were good for nothing until I started splitting cakes), or some other stable object. Place your other hand on top of the cake to stabilize it. Sprinkle the cake with granulated or confectioners' sugar if it seems as though your hand may stick to the cake surface. Slice through the cake on a perfectly hori-

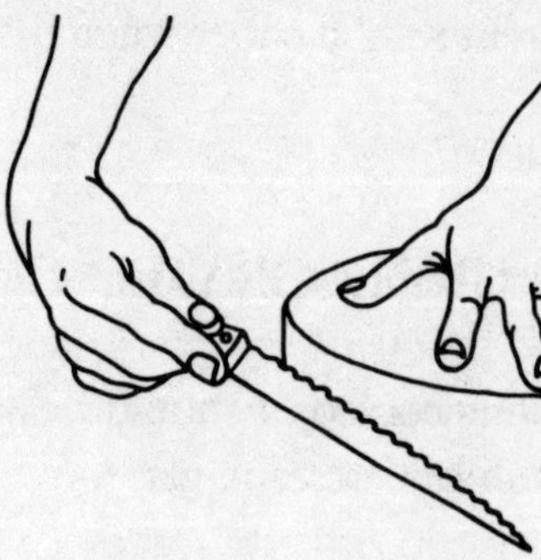

zontal plane. This is easy to accomplish if your elbow does not move. Brush away any crumbs.

### *Using a Revolving Cake Decorating Stand*

Professional revolving pedestaled cake decorating stands are available, or use a lazy Susan, revolving spice shelf, or invert a cake pan on a smaller and slightly taller pan. Work at the most comfortable height; for most people this is slightly higher than waist level. Raise the cake stand with a telephone book if too low, or put on a lower table if too high. Professionals do not place the cake on the serving platter until after it is fully decorated. However, if the prospect of transferring a fully decorated cake from one surface to another makes you nervous, position the undecorated cake directly on the serving platter before it is decorated. Strips of wax paper can be placed under the cake around the edges of the platter and removed after the cake is decorated.

### *Preparing the Cake Surface*

If the sides of the cake are uneven, shave with a very sharp knife. If the top of the cake is uneven, shave or press it down with an inverted cake pan or other flat object. Brush away all crumbs.

### *Sprinkling Liqueur or Syrup on a Cake*

Liqueurs or liqueur syrups improve the flavor of any cake and act as a preservative. The actual amount of liqueur to use is a matter of preference; two tablespoons may suffice, but some cakes and palates can tolerate and enjoy six to eight tablespoons.

Apply the liqueur or syrup onto the cake with a plant sprayer or atomizer, or sprinkle with your fingers. If the price of liqueurs is too dear to use them straight, or if the cake is to be served to children, sprinkle a syrup onto the cake. To make the syrup, boil one part water to one part sugar with a little orange or lemon rind; cool and add one-third part liqueur. Store well sealed in the refrigerator.

## • MAKING DECORATIONS •

### *Glaze*

Chocolate glaze provides an elegant, sleek, shiny surface. Glaze is made from high-quality chocolate with a little added fat—butter, cream, or both—to make the chocolate more pourable. Glaze is poured directly onto the cake and is self-leveling. Carve or level the cake to the exact shape desired, and be sure to brush away all crumbs, as the glaze will conform to the exact shape; it will not cover any imperfections. If the sides of your cake are a little wavy and you have some leftover buttercream or glaze in the refrigerator, "sculpt" the cake with it until the sides are straight. Basic chocolate glaze can be made either by melting all the ingredients together in the top of the double boiler or by heating the butter and cream to the boiling point and pouring it over the chopped chocolate. Allow the glaze to cool until it is pourable—about 94°F. It must be neither too cool (stiff) nor too hot (runny). Test the glaze by spooning a little over the cake; if it sets smoothly and evenly on the cake, it is at the correct temperature. Work near a burner when glazing in case the chocolate becomes too cool. When slightly cooled, glaze can be piped through a pastry bag for written letters and abstract designs. Excess glaze may be stored and added to the next batch. Strain the glaze through a wire mesh strainer, seal, and store it in the refrigerator. Reheat the glaze in a double boiler. Store glaze-decorated cakes, well sealed, at room temperature.

### *Making Buttercream*

For the separate components of buttercream to homogenize properly they must be at almost the same temperature and consistency when mixed. The butter must be slightly soupy, but not melted. Do not beat the buttercream too much after the components are homogenized unless you prefer a lighter color and airier consistency. If the buttercream is too runny to spread, place it in the refrigerator, stirring it occasionally to equalize the temperature. Store excess buttercream, well sealed, in the refrigerator. Allow it to sit at room temperature until it reaches the desired spreading consistency. Coffee buttercreams are better if used immediately and may separate if stored in the refrigerator. Store buttercream-decorated cakes, well sealed, in the refrigerator.

### *Whipped Cream*

Whipped cream—*Crème Chantilly*—is a quick and easy decoration. Add sugar, granulated or confectioners', and liqueur to taste; for 2 cups unwhipped cream, 2 tablespoons sugar and 1 teaspoon liqueur should be enough. In warmer months, place the whipping bowl and utensil in the freezer for a few minutes prior to whipping the cream. Whip cream only until spreadable; *do not overwhip* or cream loses its fine texture and delicacy. If cream is only slightly overwhipped, fold in a little cold liquid cream to obtain a better texture. Store whipped-cream-decorated cakes, well sealed, in the refrigerator away from pungent foodstuffs, as whipped cream readily absorbs foreign odors and flavors.

### *Mousse au Chocolat*

Mousse is a delicious filling for cakes, offering a creamy textural contrast and rich flavor. Do not freeze mousse itself, but after the mousse is spread between the layers, the cake may be frozen. Make the mousse ahead of time as the flavor is better after it has set in the refrigerator, well sealed, at least a day.

### *Crème Pâtissière*

Crème Pâtissière is a wonderful filling for cakes with fruit and is the basis for charlottes. It should not be frozen but will keep about a week, well sealed, in the refrigerator. Always smell Crème Pâtissière after it has been stored for a few days to make sure it has not gone sour.

### *Fruit Glazes*

Fruit used as a garnish should be glazed to bring out color and flavor. To add extra flavor and to improve the keeping qualities of the cake, brush a little fruit glaze over a cake before decorating it. To make a fruit glaze, strain the solids out of preserves or marmalade, use a prepared jelly, or purée preserves. Honey can also be used. Heat the glaze a little if it is not readily absorbed into the cake.

## • DECORATING TECHNIQUES •

### *How to Glaze a Cake*

For a professionally perfect surface, a cake should be "crumb-coated" before glazing. Put 1/4 cup glaze in the refrigerator until it is the consistency of buttercream, or use leftover buttercream. Spread it over the cake, sculpting perfect 90° angles at the sides. Then, place the cake on a cooling rack resting on a baking sheet to catch the excess. If the cake is very moist or dense, place it on a corrugated cardboard

cake support that has been sprinkled with sugar and then place on the rack. Pour the glaze directly onto the cake. If the glaze seems at all lumpy, pour it through a strainer. Lift the rack one inch off the baking sheet and gently drop it; repeat one or two times until the glaze has run down and covered the sides of the cake. Glaze should be completely self-leveling, requiring no spreading with a palette knife; but if the glaze seems to puddle up or does not completely cover the sides of the cake, level it with a single stroke of a palette knife. Allow the glazed cake to sit on the rack undisturbed for about 5 minutes, or until the glaze seems slightly set. To transfer to the serving platter, slide a palette knife or a broad flat spatula underneath the cake and then gently move it off the rack.

### *Decorating a Cake with Buttercream*

Allow the buttercream to reach the proper spreading consistency; this is a function of temperature. Place a little buttercream on the end of the palette knife, then anchor your elbow against your body, your hipbone, or any other stable object. Hold the palette knife flush to the sides of the cake and spread the buttercream evenly over the sides. A more even surface is achieved by holding the knife stable and revolving the cake than vice versa. To make a neat edge, level off excess buttercream at a 90° (right) angle to the sides. Spread a lot of buttercream over the top of the cake and level off the excess by revolving the cake stand. You should now have a perfectly smooth cake with a flat top and perpendicular sides. Be as quick and efficient as possible; the buttercream will liquefy when frictional heat is generated by excessive spreading.

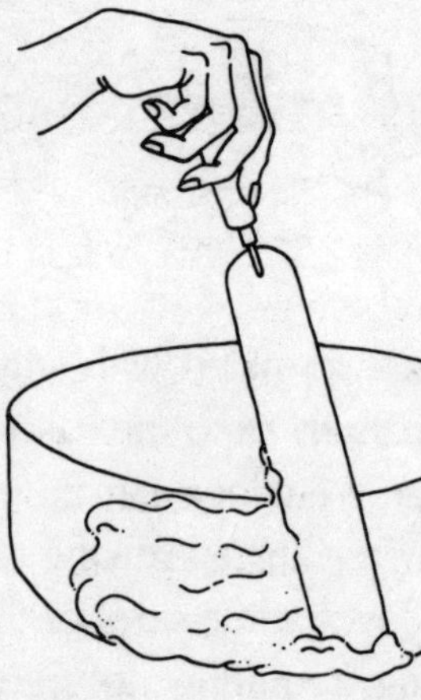

## *Decorating a Cake with Whipped Cream*

Follow the same guidelines as for buttercream. Be very fast and efficient; do not work the whipped cream too much; whipped cream can turn to butter merely through the spreading action.

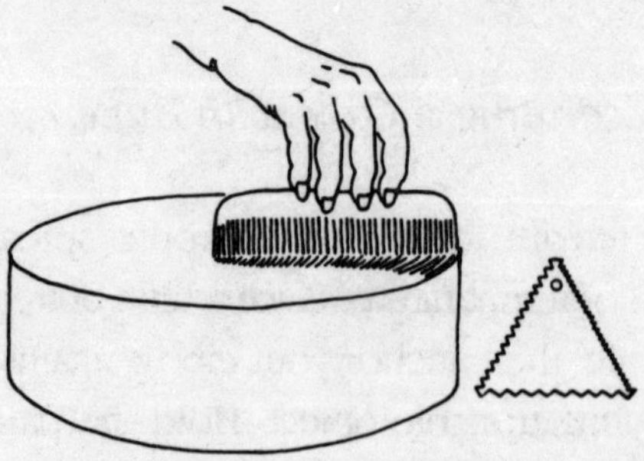

*Texturing a Cake*

A decorating comb can be used to score the sides of a glazed, or buttercream- or whipped-cream-decorated cake. Anchor your arm, hold the comb flush to the side of the cake, and revolve the cake stand (holding the comb stable) or simply texture the cake with the comb in a random fashion.

## • USING A PASTRY BAG •

Squeezing a substance through a pastry bag is called piping or forcing. A plastic coupling can be fitted through the inside of the bag, a tip pressed against the coupling and then fastened with a plastic nut fastener, or you can simply insert the pastry tip into the bag without a coupling and nut fastener. The advantage of using the coupling method is that the tips can be changed without cleaning the pastry bag.

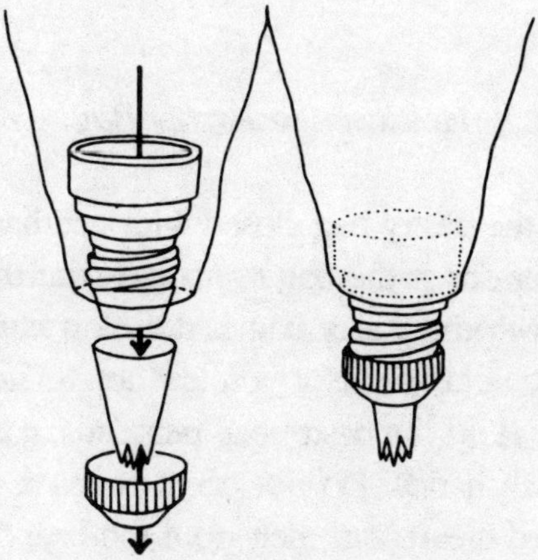

*Filling the Pastry Bag*

Stand the pastry bag up in a jar and spoon in the filling, or simply hold the pastry bag with the top widely open in one hand and spoon the filling in with the other hand, leaving at least a 2-inch margin on top for folding the bag over. Refilling a pastry bag is messy; fill it to capacity the first time unless filling it with a very body-heat-sensitive mixture such as buttercream or whipped cream. Fold over or twist the top of the pastry bag closed so that the mixture does not come out the wrong end.

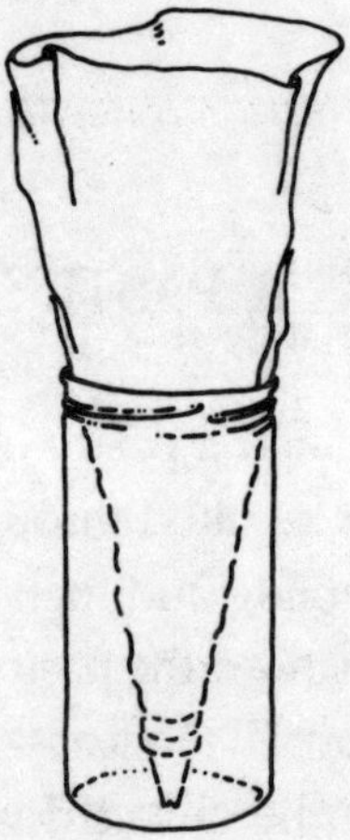

*Holding the Pastry Bag*

Hold the end of the pastry bag closed with one hand and place the other hand farther down the bag to squeeze out the mixture. Make sure you work with the pastry bag at the most comfortable height; make appropriate adjustments if you are not. Stand balanced, both feet on the floor. Hold the pastry bag perpendicular to the cake. Relax. Do not clench hands. Do not exert excessive pressure. Buttercream or whipped cream can melt from the heat of tense, nervous hands. Practice decorating an inverted cake pan with mashed potatoes. Do not be dismayed if your pastry bag technique is not perfect on your first attempts. You are not born knowing how to use a pastry bag; you will learn through practice.

### *Piping Meringue*

Fit a pastry bag with a ½-inch plain nozzle and fill it to capacity. Fill in the outlines traced on the prepared wax or parchment paper, beginning at the outer perimeter and working your way around in a spiral toward the center.

### *Piping Ladyfingers*

Fit a pastry bag with a ½-inch plain nozzle and fill to capacity. Pipe the batter into approximately 1-by-6-inch strips onto the prepared wax or parchment paper, allowing at least ½ inch between the ladyfingers.

### *Piping Cream Puff Mixture*

Fit the pastry bag with a ¾- to 1-inch plain nozzle and fill to capacity. Pipe balls approximately 1 to 1½ inches in diameter. Allow at least 1 inch between the balls. If the tips of the cream puffs stick up, push them down with your finger or a wet knife.

### *Filling Cream Puffs*

Pierce the undersides of the baked and cooled cream puffs with a knife. Fit a pastry bag with a ½-inch plain nozzle and fill to capacity with the filling mixture. Pipe the filling into the cream puffs through the opening made by the knife.

### *Writing or Decorating with Molten Chocolate Glaze*

Fit a small pastry bag with a writing tip and fill with a small amount of glaze (about ¼ cup); a little goes a long way. Practice the word, words, or abstract design on a tabletop or wax paper to determine how and where they should fit on the cake. Writing with chocolate glaze must be rapidly executed and is best suited to a flowing free-form script. Do not attempt formal letters or decoration styles with molten chocolate glaze. Celebrate the flowing nature of the material; delight in dribbling the glaze with wanton abandon.

### *The Spider Web Effect*

This is an easy technique for a dramatic and dynamic design. It looks best when the color of the glaze is in contrast to the color of the buttercream. Fit a pastry bag with a writing tip and fill it with about 1/4 cup of chocolate glaze.

METHOD I: Draw a free-hand spiral with the molten chocolate glaze or put the cake on a revolving cake stand, position the writing tip in the center of the cake, and spin the cake stand while moving your hand out toward the edge. Drag the point of a knife lightly along the surface of the cake through the glaze, drawing radii alternately, starting from the center and then from the edge of the cake.

METHOD II: Draw several parallel lines across the cake surface. Drag the point of a knife lightly along the surface of the cake through the glaze, alternately starting from opposite sides of the cake as if drawing a series of S shapes.

### *Piping Buttercream and Whipped-Cream Borders*

Fit a pastry bag with any plain or fanciful tip and fill it only half full. As buttercream and whipped cream melt with friction caused by body heat, it is better to fill the pastry bag halfway twice. Practice with mashed potatoes on the table or countertop to get into the rhythm of piping a border. Do not think about the exact form of the border, but only the rhythm and the spacing. Pipe designs with your eyes closed. Do not forget to breathe; do not clench your teeth; do not forget the fun of what you are doing.

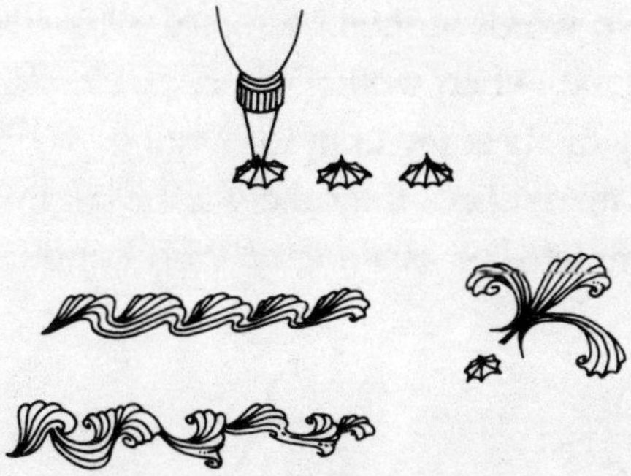

### *Designing an Ornamental Scheme for a Cake*

When you feel confident in your piping technique, approach the design problem. Rather than looking at cake-decorating manuals that always emphasize the kitschy and overdone, consider design principles from other art forms such as sho-ka, Japanese flower arranging; or bonsai, Japanese miniature tree arrangements. Strive for a design growing out of the basic structure of the cake; let the nature of the materials determine the ornamental form; choose a dynamic but restful design. As Frank Lloyd Wright wrote in *The Future of Architecture*, ornament should be "*of* the thing, not *on* it. Emotional in its nature, ornament is—if well conceived—not only the *poetry* but *is the character of the structure revealed and enhanced*. If not well conceived, architecture [or a confection] is destroyed by ornament."

When I first learned to use a pastry bag, I was infatuated with the new tool and piled cakes with brightly colored flowers. Now my style has evolved from an immature flamboyance and fascination with the bizarre to a quiet simplicity; the same *chef pâtissière* who once made bright green roses with red leaves when bored now finds meaning in almost geometric simplicity. A border of shapes each perfectly formed is more appropriate than a dizzying, complex, and elaborate border.

Only one or two words written on top of a cake can be integrated into a design scheme. When writing, choose a simple letter style; buttercream is hardly the best medium for writing.

Consider how many slices the cake will be cut into. Consider the advantage of symmetry or asymmetry. Also consider what colored

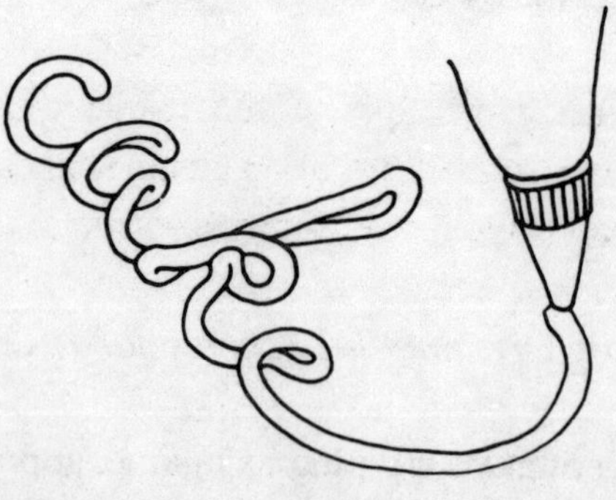

garnishes may accompany the border design. Further, consider the proportion of the cake and how a border design will change it. Walk around the cake to see it from many different angles. If symmetry of design is important, measure and make slight indentations at critical points.

## • GARNISHES •

### *Fruit*

The color of some fruits set against chocolate or whipped cream makes a very attractive garnish. Do not prepare the garnishing fruit until immediately before serving the cake; some fruits can discolor and their flavors will dissipate. Strawberries, raspberries, kiwi fruit, blueberries, and citrus fruit can be used uncooked. Pears should be poached. Lay the pear half flat and slice into 1/8-inch segments. Allow the poached fruit to drain on a rack or a towel so the excess liquid does not drip onto the cake, making it look very sloppy. For a stunning appearance, glaze the garnishing fruit. Strain preserves, marmalade, or use a clear jelly or honey and brush it onto the fruit, or dip the fruit into it. Allow the glazed fruit to drain before placing it on the cake.

### *Candied Citrus Rind*

Candied Citrus Rind (see page 129) glistens like jewels against a background of chocolate. Cut the rind into fanciful shapes with pinking shears or small canapé cutters; the possibilities are as extensive as your imagination.

### *Chocolate Curls*

"Peel" a block of room-temperature bittersweet chocolate with a potato peeler or pear corer, letting the curls fall onto a piece of wax paper. Do not touch the curls with your hands; body heat may melt them. Place the curls on the cake with a palette knife. Do not store these garnishes; make and use immediately.

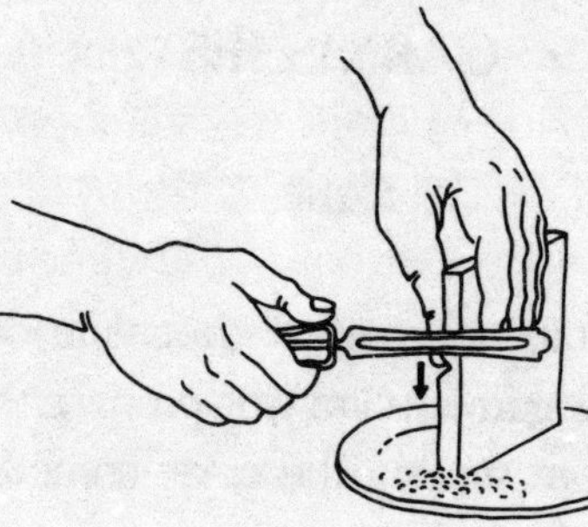

*Chocolate Cigarettes*

These dainties look more like cinnamon bark to me, but "cigarettes" is what they are commonly called. Melt bittersweet chocolate (3 ounces will make about thirty 2½-inch-long cigarettes). Depending on the particular chocolate used, adding a little cocoa butter (available in pharmacies) or flavorless vegetable (not olive) oil may be necessary (1 teaspoon to 3 ounces of chocolate works well). Spread the chocolate thinly on a piece of marble; 1/16 of an inch is the optimum thickness. Allow the chocolate to cool but not become brittle; about 10 minutes at a cool room temperature should be enough. Score into 2½-inch lengths. With a putty knife, square-edged metal scraper, or chef's knife (at a 45° angle) scrape the chocolate into rolls. Score the chocolate after rolling about 1 inch. Remove the cigarettes with the knife or scraper to a plate or set directly on the cake. Chocolate cigarettes can shatter just like cinnamon bark; exercise extreme gentleness. If this operation is not successful, the chocolate may have been at the wrong temperature; allow it to cool a little more, or remelt the chocolate and try again, not allowing it to cool quite so much. As these garnishes are very delicate, they should not be stored; use immediately.

### *Chocolate Leaves*

Wash and pat dry leaves at least one inch long from unsprayed, nonpoisonous plants; rose leaves work well. Melt bittersweet chocolate (3 ounces will make about twenty-four 1-inch-long leaves) and spread it over the back side of the leaves with a palette knife, being careful not to get any of the chocolate on the front side. Place chocolate-side-up on a baking sheet or plate. Allow the chocolate to harden; about 10 minutes at a cool room temperature or 5 minutes in the refrigerator should be enough. Gently peel away the leaves. Touch only on the underside, as the chocolate is vulnerable to fingerprints that spoil their appearance. As they are very delicate, chocolate leaves should be used immediately and not stored.

### *Chocolate Lace*

Line a baking sheet with wax paper or parchment. Fit a pastry bag with a writing tip and fill with about 3 ounces of slightly cooled melted bittersweet chocolate. Pipe a series of extending isosceles triangles each with the same apex or a series of loops each with the same base point. Allow the glaze to harden for about 10 minutes at a cool room temperature or about 5 minutes in the refrigerator. Gently loosen the lace from the paper with a palette knife and place directly onto the cake. Handle only on the backside; the chocolate is vulnerable to fingerprints that spoil the appearance.

### *Nuts*

Nuts make a simple and attractive garnish. Use whole unblanched or blanched almonds separately or in combination. Hazelnuts, macadamia nuts, half walnuts, or pecans dress up a cake also. Sliced almonds can be pressed into the sides of a cake, or sprinkled over the

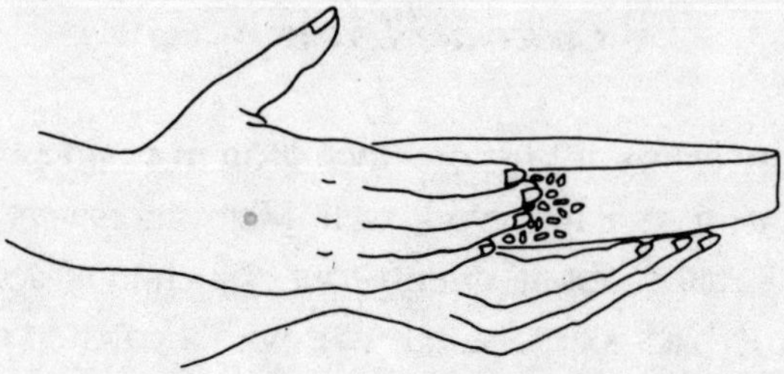

entire cake. If using a cardboard cake support, lift the cake, then take a handful of nuts and press them into the sides of the cake. Hold your hand flush to the cake, allowing the excess nuts to fall away. If the cake is very fragile or you do not care to pick it up, take a handful of nuts and press them into the sides of the cake, moving your hand around the cake. Brush away any excess nuts.

## *Candy*

Colorful hard candies or jelly beans can dress up a chocolate surface. Chocolate "coffee beans" also are attractive on cakes in which coffee is a component (see photograph of Pecan, Cocoa, and Coffee Torte with Bourbon and Mocha Buttercream).

## *Fresh Flowers*

The natural colors of fresh flowers are a dramatic contrast to chocolate and whipped-cream surfaces and are infinitely more beautiful than fake flowers rendered in buttercream or marzipan. Choose small flowers. Rosebuds are very beautiful on a cake, but more unusual flowers can be equally attractive, such as orchids, cornflowers, or even daisies. Flowers can complement a buttercream border or can be the solo ornamentation on a cake. Of course, flowers should be removed before cutting the cake.

## • SERVING AND STORAGE •

### *Cutting a Cake*

Cut a cake with a very sharp knife, preferably with a narrow blade. Drier cakes respond well to serrated knives. Cut cleanly in one motion, if possible.

### *Serving a Cake*

Gently slide a broad flat tool under the slice of cake and transfer it to the serving plate.

### *Storing Buttercream-Decorated Cakes*

Store buttercream-decorated cakes, well sealed, in the refrigerator. Allow the cake to come to room temperature before serving, as the flavors are most active at a warmer temperature.

### *Storing Whipped-Cream-Decorated Cakes*

Store whipped-cream-decorated cakes, well sealed, in the refrigerator.

### *Storing Glaze-Decorated Cakes*

Store glaze-decorated cakes, well sealed, at room temperature. The glaze will "bloom" (the cocoa butter in the chocolate will rise to the surface in little white spots) if it is refrigerated.

## • TRANSPORTING CAKES •

It is better to allow someone else to transport your fragile culinary creations and remain blissfully ignorant as to whether or not they arrived at their destination intact. However, if you are very brave, or have no choice but to transport your own cake, do not panic. Place the cake inside a box with a clearance of at least ½ to 1 inch on all sides. Stuff crumpled paper into the corners of the box, allowing it to touch the cake plate or support but not the cake itself. The cake will be able to shift a little if necessary, but will not smash against the sides of the box. To be doubly secure, place the box inside another box 2 to 3 inches larger all around. Wrap a towel or crumpled paper around the inside box to absorb shocks. Remember always to carry the cake level.

# PLAIN CAKES

## • ABOUT THE GÉNOISE •

Génoise is *the* classic sponge cake—simple, subtle, and sublime. The word means "from Genoa" (Italy). Perhaps Catherine de Medici's chefs brought the cake to France, but no one knows the precise origin of the name. The batter is beautiful and will seem alive with air bubbles. Like many other batters and doughs, the batter is better when made in two or more batches at a time; the action of beating the eggs works better in larger amounts up to a point. Remember that the size of the bowl used for beating the eggs must be at least six times the volume of the liquid mixture before it is beaten. If you do not possess an electric mixer, this cake is difficult, but not impossible. In the old days, children, husbands, and neighbors were gathered around to take turns beating génoise mixtures. Hand beating takes 25 to 30 minutes.

Génoise is an expressive cake in a way that goes beyond taste; when it is finished baking, it will tell you. A wonderful buttery smell exudes from the oven.

The following recipes are for two cakes, because it is difficult, if not impossible, to beat the eggs properly in small batches. Génoises go stale quickly, but can be successfully frozen for 1 to 2 weeks; wrap very securely.

# *Génoise Simple*

The classic sponge cake.

• *2 cakes, 8 to 10 servings each* •

1 cup (4 to 5 large) eggs
2/3 cup (5 1/2 ounces) sugar
1 1/2 cups sifted and then measured (6 ounces) cake flour
1/4 cup (2 ounces) unsalted butter, melted

Preheat oven to 325°F.

Butter two 8-inch round pans, or any pans holding 4 cups of water each. Line them with wax paper, butter the paper, and flour the pans.

Whisk the eggs and the sugar in a heavy mixing bowl set over simmering, but not boiling, water, until the mixture is too hot to keep your finger in for more than a second (125°F.). Remove from the heat and beat at a high speed with an electric mixer until the mixture is thick and ribbonlike, 5 to 10 minutes. Fold in the flour, a third at a time, while trickling in the butter. Do this as quickly as possible. Mix only until smooth. *Do not overmix.* Divide the batter equally between the prepared pans and bake until the cakes are dry on top and start to shrink away from the sides of the pans, about 25 minutes. Cool 2 minutes in the pans, then gently invert onto a cooling rack.

# *Génoise au Chocolat*

A light sponge cake made with cocoa.

• *2 cakes, 8 to 10 servings each* •

2 tablespoons (1/2 ounce) cocoa, packed
1 1/2 cups sifted and then measured (6 ounces) cake flour

1 cup (4 to 5 large) eggs
⅔ cup (5½ ounces) sugar

Preheat oven to 325°F.

Butter two 8-inch round pans, or any pans holding 4 cups of water each. Line them with wax paper, butter the paper, and flour the pans.

Sift the cocoa and flour together twice; set aside. Whisk the eggs and the sugar in a heavy mixing bowl set over simmering, but not boiling, water, until the mixture is too hot to keep your finger in for more than a second (125°F.). Remove from the heat and beat at a high speed with an electric mixer until the mixture is thick and ribbonlike, 5 to 10 minutes. Fold in the cocoa/flour mixture a third at a time. Do this as quickly as possible. Mix only until smooth. *Do not overmix.* Divide the batter equally between the prepared pans and bake until the cakes are dry on top and start to shrink away from the sides of the pans, about 20 to 25 minutes. Cool 2 minutes in the pans, then gently invert onto a cooling rack.

# *Honey Génoise au Chocolat*

Suspend your disbelief, seasoned skeptics, it works!

• *2 cakes, 8 to 10 servings each* •

2 tablespoons (½ ounce) cocoa, packed
1½ cups sifted and then measured (6 ounces) cake flour
1 cup (4 to 5 large) eggs
½ cup (6 ounces) honey

Preheat oven to 325°F.

Butter two 8-inch round pans, or any pans holding 4 cups of water each. Line them with wax paper, butter the paper, and flour the pans.

Follow the procedure for the Génoise au Chocolat (preceding recipe), substituting honey for the sugar.

# *Ladyfingers*

Spongy little oblong cakes used in making a charlotte.

• *16, enough for a charlotte* •

2 large eggs, separated (1/4 cup whites, 1/6 cup yolks)
1/3 cup (2 1/2 ounces) sugar
1/2 cup sifted and then measured (2 ounces) cake flour

Preheat oven to 375°F.

Butter and sprinkle with granulated sugar one 12-by-18-inch baking sheet lined with wax paper.

Beat the egg whites with half the sugar until the peaks keep their shape; set aside. Beat the egg yolks with the remaining sugar until

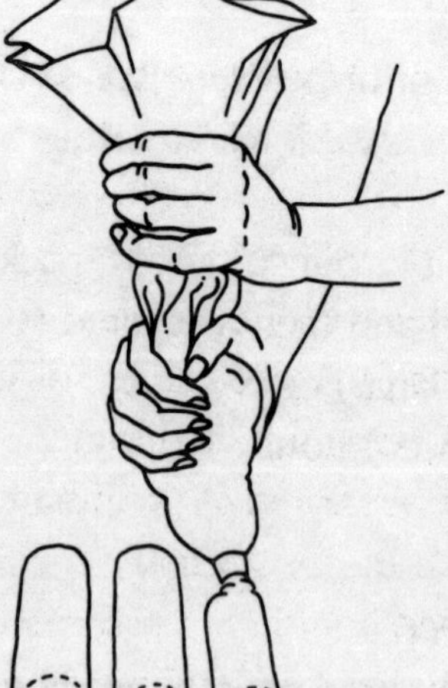

thick and ribbonlike. Alternately, a third at a time, fold the beaten egg whites and the flour into the beaten egg yolks. Mix only until smooth. *Do not overmix.* Put the batter in a pastry bag fitted with a ½-inch nozzle tip. Pipe 16 ladyfingers, 4 to 5 inches long and ½ to ¾ inch wide. Sprinkle each ladyfinger with granulated sugar and bake until slightly spongy and dry, but not brown and crisp, about 8 to 10 minutes. Cool on the baking sheet. Store, refrigerated, in an airtight tin box.

## *Chocolate Ladyfingers*

Substitute 1 tablespoon cocoa for 1 tablespoon of the flour in the preceding recipe. Sift the cocoa and flour together twice before folding them into the batter.

## *Dense, Moist Chocolate Cake*

A simple chocolate cake that may be used as a base for many other creations.

• *10 to 12 servings* •

4 ounces bittersweet chocolate
2 tablespoons (1 ounce) coffee or liqueur
½ cup (4 ounces) unsalted butter
3 large eggs, separated (⅓ cup whites, ¼ cup yolks)
⅔ cup (5½ ounces) sugar
1¼ cups sifted and then measured (5 ounces) cake flour
Chocolate Buttercream (following recipe)

Preheat oven to 325°F.

Butter one 8-inch round pan, or any pan holding 4 cups of water. Line it with wax paper, butter the paper, and flour the pan.

In the top of a double boiler, over hot, but not simmering, water, melt the chocolate, stirring in the coffee or liqueur and butter; set aside. Beat the egg whites with ⅓ cup of the sugar until the peaks keep their shape; set aside. Beat the egg yolks with the remaining ⅓ cup sugar until thick and ribbonlike. Fold the chocolate mixture into the beaten egg yolks. Alternately, a third at a time, fold the beaten egg whites and the flour into the chocolate mixture. Mix only until smooth. *Do not overmix.*

Pour the batter into the prepared pan and bake until a knife inserted into the center of the cake comes out clean, about 30 minutes. Cool 2 minutes in the pan, then gently invert onto a cooling rack.

Split the cake into 2 or 3 layers, fill, and decorate with Chocolate Buttercream.

# Chocolate Buttercream

This buttercream is rich and velvety without being cloyingly sweet.

• *Enough to fill and decorate one 8- to 10-inch cake* •

5 ounces bittersweet chocolate
2 tablespoons (1 ounce) coffee or liqueur
½ cup (4 ounces) sugar
½ cup (2 to 3 large) eggs
1 cup (8 ounces) unsalted butter, at room temperature

In the top of a double boiler, over hot, but not simmering, water, melt the chocolate with the coffee or liqueur; set aside. In the top of a double boiler, over simmering, but not boiling, water, whisk the sugar and eggs until very thick and the whisk marks keep their shape (125°F.). Remove from the heat. Fold the chocolate into the eggs. Beat in the butter chunk by chunk until very smooth. Chill until the desired spreading consistency is obtained.

# Buttermilk Chocolate Cake

A classic American variation on the chocolate cake theme.

• *10 to 12 servings* •

3 ounces unsweetened chocolate
½ cup (4 ounces) unsalted butter
1 cup (8 ounces) buttermilk
3 large eggs, separated (⅓ cup whites, ¼ cup yolks)
1½ cups (12 ounces) sugar
1 cup sifted and then measured (4 ounces) cake flour

♠ ♠ ♠

2 cups (16 ounces) whipping cream
3 tablespoons (1½ ounces) sugar
1 to 2 teaspoons liqueur kirsch (optional)
Chocolate Curls, page 69

Preheat oven to 325°F.

Butter two 8-inch round pans, or any pans holding 4 cups of water each. Line them with wax paper, butter the paper, and flour the pans.

In the top of a double boiler, over hot, not simmering, water, melt the chocolate. Stir in the butter and buttermilk and set aside. Beat the egg whites with 1 cup of the sugar until the peaks keep their shape;

set aside. Beat the egg yolks with the remaining ½ cup sugar until thick and ribbonlike. Fold the chocolate mixture into the beaten egg yolks. Alternately, a third at a time, fold the beaten egg whites and the flour into the chocolate mixture. Mix only until smooth. *Do not overmix.* Divide the batter equally between the prepared pans and bake until dry on top, about 30 minutes. Cool 2 minutes in the pans, then gently invert onto a cooling rack. When completely cooled, split the layers if desired (see page 56).

Whip the cream with 3 tablespoons sugar and liqueur kirsch, if desired. Assemble the layers with the whipped cream between them and decorate the cake with the remaining whipped cream. Press the Chocolate Curls into the whipped cream on the top and sides of the cake.

# *Chocolate Crumb Torte*

Save the stale ends of cakes or *succès pas* (unsuccessful) cakes and recycle them into this surprisingly good torte. See page 52 for the method of preparing the crumbs.

• *10 to 12 servings* •

1 cup (6 ounces) chocolate cake crumbs, packed
½ cup (2 ounces) finely ground walnuts or almonds
2 tablespoons (½ ounce) cocoa, packed
4 large eggs, separated (½ cup whites, ⅓ cup yolks)
½ cup (4 ounces) sugar
Chocolate Glaze (following recipe)

Preheat oven to 325°F.

Butter one 9-inch round springform pan, or any pan holding 6

*Chocolate Raspberry Torte (page 145); Pavlova (page 134);*
*Chocolate Nectarine Cake (page 132)*

*Clockwise from top: Chocolate-Almond Torte with Citrus and Spices (page 153) and Chocolate Glaze (page 85); Pecan, Cocoa, and Coffee Torte (page 160) with Bourbon and Mocha Buttercream (page 161); Chocolate Burgundy Pear Cake (page 137); Dense Moist Chocolate Cake (page 81) with Chocolate Buttercream (page 82)*

cups of water. Line it with wax paper, butter the paper, and flour the pan.

Mix the crumbs and nuts. Sift the cocoa into them and set aside. Beat the egg whites with 1/4 cup of the sugar until the peaks keep their shape; set aside. Beat the egg yolks with the remaining 1/4 cup sugar until thick and ribbonlike. Alternately, a third at a time, fold the beaten egg whites and the crumb mixture into the beaten egg yolks. Mix only until smooth. *Do not overmix.* Pour the batter into the prepared pan and bake until a knife inserted into the center of the torte comes out clean, about 35 minutes. Loosen the springform and cool for 10 minutes. Gently invert onto a piece of cardboard cut to the size of the torte and sprinkled with sugar.

Decorate with Chocolate Glaze.

# *Chocolate Glaze*

This glaze gives any cake an elegant, classical look.

• *Enough for one 8- to 9-inch cake* •

6 ounces bittersweet chocolate, grated
2 tablespoons and 2 teaspoons (1 2/3 ounces) whipping cream
2 tablespoons (1 ounce) unsalted butter

METHOD I: In the top of a double boiler, over hot, but not simmering, water, melt the chocolate and cream. Remove from the heat and stir in the butter.

METHOD II: Bring the cream and butter to a boil and immediately pour them over the chocolate. Stir like mad to make sure the chocolate does not burn before it is melted.

# *Chocolate Malt Cake*

Here is a cake with the old-fashioned taste of a chocolate malted. Malt is available in health-food stores and some supermarkets.

• *8 to 10 servings* •

2 ounces bittersweet chocolate
½ cup (4 ounces) unsalted butter
¼ cup (2 ounces) malt extract
2 tablespoons (1 ounce) water or coffee
4 large eggs, separated (½ cup whites, ⅓ cup yolks)
½ cup (4 ounces) sugar
1 cup sifted and then measured (4 ounces) cake flour
Chocolate Buttercream, page 82

Preheat oven to 325°F.

Butter two 8-inch round pans, or any pans holding 4 cups of water each. Line them with wax paper, butter the paper, and flour the pans.

In the top of a double boiler, over hot, but not simmering, water, melt the chocolate, butter, and malt extract with the water or coffee; set aside. Beat the egg whites with ¼ cup of sugar until the peaks keep their shape; set aside. Beat the egg yolks with the remaining ¼ cup sugar until thick and ribbonlike. Fold the chocolate mixture into the beaten egg yolks. Alternately, a third at a time, fold the beaten egg whites and the flour into the chocolate mixture. Mix only until smooth. *Do not overmix.* Divide the batter equally between the prepared pans and bake until the cakes start to shrink away from the sides of the pans and a knife inserted into the center comes out clean, about 25 minutes. Cool 2 minutes in the pans, then gently invert onto a cooling rack.

Decorate with Chocolate Buttercream.

# *Chocolate Sponge Torte*

Light but very flavorful.

• *10 to 12 servings* •

4 ounces bittersweet chocolate
2 tablespoons (1 ounce) water or coffee
4 large eggs, separated (½ cup whites, ⅓ cup yolks)
⅓ cup (2½ ounces) sugar
⅜ cup sifted and then measured (3 ounces) cake flour

♠ ♠ ♠

2 to 3 tablespoons (1 to 1½ ounces) liqueur kirsch
½ cup (6 ounces) apricot, raspberry, or plum jam
Cocoa
Confectioners' sugar

Preheat oven to 325°F.

Butter one 9-inch round pan, or any pan holding 6 cups of water. Line it with wax paper, butter the paper, and flour the pan.

In the top of a double boiler, over hot, but not simmering, water, melt the chocolate with the water or coffee; set aside. Beat the egg whites with the sugar until the peaks keep their shape; set aside. Beat the egg yolks until thick. Fold the chocolate into the beaten egg yolks. Alternately, a third at a time, fold the beaten egg whites and flour into the chocolate mixture. Mix only until smooth. *Do not overmix.* Pour the batter into the prepared pan and bake until a knife comes out of the center of the torte clean, about 25 minutes. Cool 2 minutes in the pan, then gently invert onto a cooling rack.

When completely cool, split the torte into 2 layers. Sprinkle each layer with liqueur kirsch and assemble the layers by spreading the jam between them. Dust the top of the torte with cocoa. Place a doily on top of the cake and sprinkle with confectioners' sugar. Remove the doily.

# *Chocolate Yogurt Cake*

This cake has a wonderful sweet and tart quality.

• *8 to 10 servings* •

3 ounces unsweetened chocolate
½ cup (4 ounces) unsalted butter
3 large eggs, separated (⅓ cup whites, ¼ cup yolks)
1½ cups (12 ounces) sugar
1 cup (8 ounces) whole milk yogurt
1 cup sifted and then measured (4 ounces) cake flour

♠ ♠ ♠

2 cups (16 ounces) whole milk yogurt, flavored if desired
¼ to ⅓ cup sugar (omit if flavored yogurt is used)
Confectioners' sugar

Preheat oven to 325°F.

Butter two 8-inch round pans, or any pans holding 4 cups of water each. Line them with wax paper, butter the paper, and flour the pans.

In the top of a double boiler, over hot, but not simmering, water, melt the chocolate, stirring in the butter; set aside. Beat the egg whites with 1 cup of the sugar until the peaks keep their shape; set aside. Beat the egg yolks with the remaining ½ cup sugar until thick and ribbonlike. Fold 1 cup yogurt and the chocolate into the beaten egg yolks. Alternately, a third at a time, fold the beaten egg whites and the flour into the chocolate mixture. Mix only until smooth. *Do not overmix*. Divide the batter equally between the prepared pans and bake until the layers start to shrink away from the sides of the pans, about 30 minutes. Cool 2 minutes in the pans, then gently invert onto a cooling rack. When completely cooled, split each layer into 2 layers (see page 56).

Mix ¼ to ⅓ cup sugar with 2 cups yogurt (if you are not using flavored yogurt) and assemble the layers by spreading the yogurt between them. Dust the top of the cake with confectioners' sugar and serve each slice of the cake with a dollop of the leftover yogurt filling.

# *Devil's Food Cake*

This cake is made with cocoa and has a slightly reddish tint caused by a chemical reaction between the baking powder and cocoa.

• *10 to 12 servings* •

1/3 cup (2 ounces) cocoa, packed
2 cups sifted and then measured (8 ounces) cake flour
1/2 teaspoon baking powder
1/4 teaspoon salt
2 large eggs, separated (1/4 cup whites, 2 1/2 tablespoons yolk)
1 1/2 cups (12 ounces) sugar
1/2 cup (4 ounces) unsalted butter, at room temperature
1 cup (8 ounces) whole milk
Chocolate Buttercream, page 82

Preheat oven to 325°F.

Butter two 8-inch round pans, or any pans holding 4 cups of water each. Line them with wax paper, butter the paper, and flour the pans.

Sift the cocoa, flour, baking powder, and salt together twice; set aside. Beat the egg whites with 3/4 cup of the sugar until the peaks keep their shape; set aside. Beat the egg yolks with the remaining 3/4 cup of the sugar until thick and ribbonlike. Alternately, a third at a time, fold the milk and the flour mixture into the beaten egg yolks. Then, fold in the beaten egg whites. Mix only until smooth. *Do not overmix.* Divide the batter between the prepared pans and bake until the cakes are dry on top and start to shrink away from the sides of the pans, about 30 minutes. Cool 2 minutes in the pans and then gently invert onto a cooling rack.

Assemble the layers by spreading Chocolate Buttercream between them and then decorate with the remaining buttercream.

# *Fudge Cake*

Stunning! A rich, incredibly chocolaty cake.

• *16 to 18 servings* •

8 ounces bittersweet chocolate
¾ cup (6 ounces) unsalted butter
5 large eggs, separated (⅝ cup whites, ⅜ cup yolks)
¾ cup (6 ounces) sugar
¾ cup sifted and then measured (3 ounces) cake flour
3 tablespoons (1½ ounces) brandy, cognac, or
  liqueur kirsch (optional)
Chocolate Glaze, page 85

Preheat oven to 325°F.

Butter one 10-inch round springform pan, or any pan holding 9 cups of water. Line it with wax paper, butter the paper, and flour the pan.

In the top of a double boiler, over hot, but not simmering, water, melt the chocolate and butter; set aside. Beat the egg whites with ½ cup of the sugar until the peaks keep their shape; set aside. Beat the egg yolks with the remaining ¼ cup of sugar until thick and ribbon-like. Fold the chocolate-butter mixture into the beaten egg yolks. Alternately, a third at a time, fold the beaten egg whites and the flour into the chocolate mixture. Pour the batter into the prepared pan. Hold the pan 1 inch above the table and drop it to evenly distribute the batter. Bake until a knife inserted into the center of the cake comes out clean, about 40 minutes. Loosen the springform and cool 15 minutes in the pan, then gently invert onto a cooling rack.

Sprinkle on the liqueur if desired. Decorate with Chocolate Glaze.

# *Gâteau de Madame*

In this Lady's Cake, the light spongy génoise contrasts with the rich but spongy chocolate mousse.

• *8 to 10 servings* •

1 Génoise au Chocolat, page 78, split into 2 layers
2 to 4 tablespoons plus 1 teaspoon liqueur kirsch
⅓ recipe Mousse au Chocolat (following recipe)
2 cups (16 ounces) whipping cream
1 tablespoon (½ ounce) sugar
Chocolate Curls, page 69

Sprinkle each layer of the génoise with the 2 to 4 tablespoons liqueur kirsch. Spread the mousse over the bottom layer. Whip the cream with the sugar and 1 teaspoon liqueur kirsch. Spread a ¼-inch layer of whipped cream over the mousse and assemble the layers. Decorate with the remaining whipped cream. Press the Chocolate Curls into the cream on the top and sides of the cake.

# *Mousse au Chocolat*

Rich and intense, but not too sweet. This can be made several days ahead of time. Indeed, its flavor improves over time.

• *4 cups* •

8 ounces bittersweet chocolate
¼ cup (2 ounces) coffee or liqueur
6 large eggs, separated (¾ cup whites, ½ cup yolks)
1 cup (8 ounces) unsalted butter, at room temperature

In the top of a double boiler, over hot, but not simmering, water, melt the chocolate and coffee or liqueur; set aside. Beat the egg whites until stiff but not dry; set aside. Add the egg yolks to the chocolate, beating until smooth; remove from the heat. Add the butter, chunk by chunk; stir until no lumps remain and the mixture is very shiny. Quickly fold in the beaten egg whites, a quarter at a time. It will appear very gritty. Cover securely with plastic and refrigerate until set, about 1 hour.

# *Honey Chocolate Cake*

Honey and chocolate are an unexpectedly delicious combination.

• *10 to 12 servings* •

4 ounces bittersweet chocolate
2 tablespoons (1 ounce) water or coffee
½ cup (4 ounces) unsalted butter
3 large eggs, separated (⅓ cup whites, ¼ cup yolks)
½ cup (6 ounces) honey
1¼ cups sifted and then measured (5 ounces) cake flour
Chocolate Honey Buttercream (following recipe) or
Chocolate Honey Glaze I and II (following recipes)

Preheat oven to 325°F.

Butter one 9-inch round pan, or any pan holding 6 cups of water. Line it with wax paper, butter the paper, and flour the pan.

In the top of a double boiler, over hot, but not simmering, water, melt the chocolate, stirring in the water or coffee and butter; set aside. Beat the egg whites with 2 tablespoons of the honey until the peaks keep their shape; set aside. Beat the egg yolks with the remaining honey until thick and ribbonlike. Fold the chocolate mixture into the beaten egg yolks. Alternately, a third at a time, fold the beaten egg whites and the flour into the chocolate mixture. Mix only until smooth. *Do not overmix.* Pour the batter into the prepared pan and bake until a knife inserted into the center of the cake comes out clean, about 35 minutes. Cool 2 minutes in the pan, then gently invert onto a cooling rack. Decorate with Chocolate Honey Buttercream or Chocolate Honey Glaze I or II.

# *Chocolate Honey Buttercream*

Honey adds flavor and smoothness to this buttercream.

• *Enough to fill and decorate one 8- to 9-inch cake* •

5 ounces bittersweet chocolate
½ cup (6 ounces) honey
½ cup (2 to 3 large) eggs
1 cup (8 ounces) unsalted butter, at room temperature

In the top of a double boiler, over hot, but not simmering, water, melt the chocolate; set aside. In the top of a double boiler, over simmering, but not boiling, water, whisk the honey and eggs until very thick and the whisk marks keep their shape (125°F.). Remove from the heat and fold in the chocolate. Beat in the butter, chunk by chunk, until very smooth. Chill until the desired spreading consistency is obtained.

# Chocolate Honey Glaze I

Surprisingly easy to make and work with.

• *Enough for one 8- to 9-inch cake* •

4 ounces unsweetened chocolate
5 tablespoons (3¾ ounces) honey
2 tablespoons (1 ounce) unsalted butter
¼ cup (2 ounces) whipping cream

In the top of a double boiler, over hot, but not simmering, water, melt the chocolate with the other ingredients. Pour through a strainer onto the cake.

# Chocolate Honey Glaze II

• *Enough for one 8- to 9-inch cake* •

6 ounces unsweetened chocolate
½ cup (6 ounces) honey
2 tablespoons (1 ounce) unsalted butter

Follow instructions in preceding recipe.

# Honey Cocoa Torte

This elegant torte is only 3/4 inch high. A 30-minute setting time is required before serving.

*• 8 to 10 servings •*

1 cup sifted and then measured (4 ounces) cake flour
6 tablespoons (1 1/2 ounces) cocoa, packed
2 large eggs, separated (1/4 cup whites, 1/6 cup yolks)
6 tablespoons (3 ounces) unsalted butter, at room temperature
1 cup (12 ounces) honey
1/2 cup (4 ounces) whole milk
Chocolate Glaze, page 85

Preheat oven to 325°F.

Butter one 9-inch round springform pan, or any pan holding 6 cups of water. Line it with wax paper, butter the paper, and flour the pan.

Sift the flour and cocoa together twice; set aside. Beat the egg whites until stiff but not dry; set aside. Beat the egg yolks, butter, 3/4 cup honey, and milk together until very smooth. Alternately, a third at a time, fold the beaten egg whites and the flour/cocoa mixture into the yolk mixture. Mix only until smooth. *Do not overmix.* Pour the batter into the prepared pan and bake until dry on top, about 30 minutes. Loosen the springform and cool 10 minutes, then gently invert onto a cooling rack. Warm 1/4 cup honey until it is spreadable. With a pastry brush, spread the honey over the top of the cake. Decorate with Chocolate Glaze. With still-molten glaze, write the word *Honey* on top of the torte.

Allow the finished torte to set at least 30 minutes before serving; this time allows the honey to steep in. This cake will remain fresh and moist several days.

# Marble Cake

This cake is based on the French *Madeleine* or the Italian *Madallena* cake and is a simple formula of equal parts (by weight) of sugar, eggs, butter, and flour (*quartre-quarts* or four-fourths). It is also known as *pound cake* in this country.

• *8 to 10 servings* •

3 ounces bittersweet chocolate
3/4 cup (3 to 4 large) eggs
3/4 cup (6 ounces) sugar
1 1/2 cups sifted and then measured (6 ounces) cake flour
3/4 cup (6 ounces) unsalted butter, melted
Confectioners' sugar

Preheat oven to 325°F.

Butter and flour a cake mold with a hole in the center that holds 8 cups of water. An indented mold such as a Kugelhopf tube pan is appropriate.

In the top of a double boiler, over hot, but not simmering, water, melt the chocolate; set aside. In a heavy mixing bowl set over simmering, but not boiling, water, whisk the eggs and sugar until they reach a very warm room temperature (100°F.) Remove from the heat and beat the eggs with the sugar until they are about the consistency of whipped cream. Alternately, a third at a time, fold in the flour and trickle in the butter. Do this very quickly, mixing only until smooth. *Do not overmix.* Pour three-fourths of the batter into the prepared pan. Fold the chocolate into the remaining fourth of the batter. Dribble the chocolate batter into the pan and then mix a little with a fork or chopstick. Bake until a knife inserted into the center of the cake comes out clean, about 40 to 45 minutes. Cool 1 minute in the pan, then gently invert onto a cooling rack.

When completely cooled, dust with confectioners' sugar.

# *Mayonnaise Chocolate Cake*

Very moist and not at all incongruous. Mayonnaise is, after all, eggs, oil, and lemon juice, none of which clashes with chocolate. Making the mayonnaise for this cake is as easy as turning an electric blender on and off.

• *10 to 12 servings* •

1 large egg (1/4 cup, scant)
1 tablespoon (1/2 ounce) lemon juice
1/2 cup (4 ounces) bland oil, such as walnut or almond

♠ ♠ ♠

3 ounces bittersweet chocolate
3 large eggs, separated (1/3 cup whites, 1/4 cup yolks)
3/4 cup (6 ounces) sugar
1 cup sifted and then measured (4 ounces) cake flour

♠ ♠ ♠

Chocolate Buttercream, page 82

Preheat oven to 325°F.

Butter two 8-inch round pans, or any pans holding 4 cups of water each. Line them with wax paper, butter the paper, and flour the pans.

To make the mayonnaise, place 1 egg, the lemon juice, and 1/4 cup of the oil in an electric blender. Blend at medium speed for 1 minute. Trickle in the remaining oil with the motor still running. Blend for another minute or until thick; set aside.

In the top of a double boiler, over hot, but not simmering, water, melt the chocolate; set aside. Beat the egg whites with 1/2 cup of the sugar until the peaks keep their shape; set aside. Beat the egg yolks with the remaining 1/4 cup sugar until thick and ribbonlike. Fold the mayonnaise and chocolate into the beaten egg yolks. Alternately, a third at a time, fold the beaten egg whites and the flour into the chocolate mixture. Mix only until smooth. *Do not overmix.* Divide the batter equally between the prepared pans and bake until a knife inserted into the center of the layers comes out clean, about 25 minutes. Cool 2 minutes in the pans, then gently invert onto a cooling rack.

Decorate with Chocolate Buttercream.

# No-Yolk Chocolate Torte

A small and simple torte created to use extra egg whites.

• *8 to 10 servings* •

3 ounces bittersweet chocolate
3 tablespoons (1½ ounces) unsalted butter
⅔ cup (about 5 large) egg whites
⅓ cup (2½ ounces) sugar
½ cup sifted and then measured (2 ounces) cake flour

♠ ♠ ♠

¼ cup (3 ounces) apricot, raspberry, or plum jam
2 tablespoons (1 ounce) liqueur kirsch
½ cup (about 3 to 4 large) egg whites
3 tablespoons (1½ ounce) sugar

Preheat oven to 350°F.

Butter one 8-inch round pan, or any pan holding 4 cups of water. Line it with wax paper, butter the paper, and flour the pan.

In the top of a double boiler, over hot, but not simmering, water, melt the chocolate and butter; set aside. Beat ⅔ cup egg whites with ⅓ cup sugar until the peaks keep their shape. Alternately, a third at a time, fold the flour and the beaten egg whites into the chocolate mixture. Mix only until smooth. *Do not overmix.* Pour the batter into the prepared pan and bake until a knife inserted into the center of the torte comes out clean and the torte starts to shrink away from the sides of the pan, about 20 minutes. Cool 2 minutes in the pan, then gently invert onto a cooling rack. Turn the oven up to 400°F.

When the torte is cool, brush on the jam and sprinkle on the liqueur kirsch. Beat ½ cup egg whites with 3 tablespoons sugar until very stiff. Place the torte on an ovenproof serving platter. Spread the meringue over the top and sides of the torte with a palette knife and make a decorative border using a pastry bag (page 35). Return the torte to the oven and bake another 10 to 15 minutes or until the meringue browns slightly along the edges. Cool 10 minutes before serving.

# *Sachertorte*

As I have never been to the Hotel Sacher in Vienna, my only feeble claim to the authenticity of this recipe is that it comes from a very reliable secondhand source! The liqueur kirsch acts as a preservative; and the cake will stay fresh for 4 to 5 days. It is best eaten after the flavors have mellowed for 2 days. Store well wrapped and unrefrigerated. Sachertorte is traditionally served with a dollop of whipped cream on the side.

• *16 servings* •

7 ounces bittersweet chocolate
½ cup (4 ounces) unsalted butter
8 large eggs, separated (1 cup whites, ⅔ cup yolks)
1 cup (8 ounces) sugar
1 cup sifted and then measured (4 ounces) cake flour

♠ ♠ ♠

½ cup (4 ounces) liqueur kirsch
½ cup (6 ounces) apricot preserves
Chocolate Glaze, page 85
1 cup (8 ounces) whipping cream
1 tablespoon sugar

Preheat oven to 325°F.

Butter one 10-inch round springform pan, or any pan holding 9 cups of water. Line it with wax paper, butter the paper, and flour the pan.

In the top of a double boiler, over hot, but not simmering, water, melt the chocolate and the butter; set aside. Beat the egg whites with ½ cup of sugar until the peaks keep their shape; set aside. Beat the egg yolks with the remaining ½ cup sugar until thick and ribbonlike. Fold the chocolate mixture into the beaten egg yolks. Alternately, a third at a time, fold the beaten egg whites and flour into the chocolate mixture. Mix only until smooth. *Do not overmix.* Pour the batter into the prepared pan and bake until a knife inserted into the center of the cake comes out clean, about 40 minutes. Loosen the springform and cool 10 minutes, then gently invert onto a cooling rack.

When completely cooled, split the cake into 2 or 3 layers. Sprinkle the liqueur kirsch on the layers and spread the apricot preserves between them.

Decorate with Chocolate Glaze. With still-molten glaze, write the word *Sacher* on top of the torte.

Whip the cream with 1 tablespoon sugar and put a generous spoonful on each serving plate.

# Sour Cream Chocolate Cake

Popularized in Jewish delicatessens, this cake has become an American favorite.

• *10 to 12 servings* •

- 3 ounces unsweetened chocolate
- 2 tablespoons (1 ounce) unsalted butter
- 3 large eggs, separated (1/3 cup whites, 1/4 cup yolks)
- 1 1/2 cups (12 ounces) sugar
- 1 cup (8 ounces) sour cream
- 1 cup sifted and then measured (4 ounces) cake flour
- Chocolate Buttercream, page 82

Preheat oven to 325°F.

Butter two 8-inch round pans, or any pans holding 4 cups of water each. Line them with wax paper, butter the paper, and flour the pans.

In the top of a double boiler, over hot, but not simmering, water, melt the chocolate, stirring in the butter; set aside. Beat the egg whites with 1 cup of the sugar until the peaks keep their shape; set aside. Beat the egg yolks with the remaining 1/2 cup sugar until thick and ribbonlike. Fold the chocolate and sour cream into the beaten egg yolks. Alternately, a third at a time, fold the beaten egg whites and the flour into the chocolate mixture. Mix only until smooth. *Do not overmix.* Divide the batter equally between the prepared pans and bake until the layers start to shrink away from the sides of the pans, about 25 minutes. Cool 2 minutes in the pans, then gently invert onto a cooling rack.

Decorate with Chocolate Buttercream.

# Turkish Chocolate Cake

A multilayered loaf cake featuring a delicious homemade coffee liqueur. Allow the finished cake to set at least 30 minutes before serving; this time allows the coffee liqueur to blend with the other flavors. This cake will remain moist and fresh for several days because of the abundance of liqueur.

• *8 to 10 servings* •

Dense, Moist Chocolate Cake, page 81, made in a baking sheet (jelly-roll pan)
6 tablespoons Coffee Liqueur (following recipe) or Kahlúa
Cocoa Kahlúa Buttercream, opposite
Chocolate Glaze, page 85

Preheat oven to 325°F.

Butter one 12-by-18-inch baking sheet. Line it with wax paper, butter the paper, and flour the pan.

Follow the recipe and procedures for the chocolate cake, but spread the batter evenly on the baking sheet instead of pouring it into the round pan. Bake until dry on top and a knife inserted into the center of the cake comes out clean, about 15 to 20 minutes. Cool on the baking sheet.

Cut the cake in half crosswise so there are two 9-by-12-inch pieces. Cut each of these pieces into thirds crosswise to get six 4-by-9-inch pieces. Sprinkle each piece with 1 tablespoon Coffee Liqueur or Kahlúa. Spread all but ⅓ cup of the Cocoa Kahlúa Buttercream on five of the layers. Assemble the cake with the plain layer on top. Trim the stack of layers with a serrated knife if there are any uneven places. Spread a little of the remaining buttercream on the sides of the cake, making it perfectly smooth. Refrigerate about 30 minutes to allow the buttercream to harden. Decorate with Chocolate Glaze. Put the rest of the buttercream in a pastry bag with a star tip and pipe a decorative border around the edge of the cake.

# *Coffee Liqueur*

Very easy and delicious. Make a double batch, put it in fancy bottles, and give as gifts.

• *Makes 1 quart* •

1¾ cups (14 ounces) water
1½ cups (12 ounces) sugar
1 vanilla bean
¾ cup (6 ounces) freshly ground coffee
2 cups (16 ounces) vodka

Bring the water, sugar, and vanilla bean to a boil. Lower the heat and simmer for 10 minutes. Remove from the heat and add the coffee. When cooled, add the vodka. Allow the mixture to set, unrefrigerated but covered, for 24 hours. Strain through a double layer of cheesecloth. Bottle in sterilized brown glass containers (such as beer or stout bottles) and seal securely. Age in a cool place away from all light for at least 2 weeks.

# *Cocoa Kahlúa Buttercream*

Light and subtle, with a hint of cocoa and Kahlúa.

• *Enough for one 8- to 9-inch cake* •

2 egg yolks (2 tablespoons)
¼ cup (4 ounces) sugar
3 tablespoons (1½ ounces) Kahlúa or Coffee Liqueur (preceding recipe)
2 tablespoons (½ ounce) cocoa, packed
1 cup (8 ounces) unsalted butter, very soft

Blend the egg yolks, sugar, and Kahlúa or Coffee Liqueur. Sift in the cocoa. In the top of a double boiler, over simmering, but not boiling, water, whisk the mixture until very thick and the whisk marks keep their shape (125°F.). Remove from the heat and, cool, add the butter, a tablespoon at a time. (It should be too soft to add chunk by chunk.) It is very important that the custard and butter are almost the same temperature and consistency when combined; otherwise the mixture will probably separate. The butter should look almost soupy.

# *Zigomar*

An exotic, multilayered loaf cake featuring pistachio nuts and liqueur kirsch. Allow the finished cake to set at least 30 minutes before serving; this time allows the liqueur kirsch to blend with the other flavors. This cake will remain moist and fresh for several days because of the abundance of liqueur.

• *8 to 10 servings* •

Dense, Moist Chocolate Cake, page 81, made in a baking sheet (jelly-roll-pan)
6 tablespoons (3 ounces) liqueur kirsch
Pistachio Buttercream (following recipe)
½ recipe Chocolate Buttercream, page 82
½ cup (2 ounces) finely chopped pistachio nuts

Preheat oven to 325°F.

Butter one 12-by-18-inch baking sheet. Line it with wax paper, butter the paper, and flour the sheet.

Follow the recipe and procedure for the chocolate cake, but spread the batter evenly on the baking sheet instead of pouring it into the round pan. Bake until dry on top and a knife inserted into the center of the sheet comes out clean, about 15 to 20 minutes. Cool on the baking sheet.

Cut the cake in half crosswise so there are two 9-by-12-inch pieces. Cut each of these pieces into thirds crosswise to get six 4-by-9-inch pieces. Sprinkle each piece with 1 tablespoon liqueur kirsch. Spread all the Pistachio Buttercream on 5 of the layers. Assemble the cake with the plain layer on top. Trim the stack of layers with a serrated knife if there are any uneven places. Spread the Chocolate Buttercream over the top and sides of the cake. Press the pistachio nuts into the buttercream on the sides of the cake.

# *Pistachio Buttercream*

Good enough to eat as candy. Roll any leftovers into balls and dust with cocoa powder.

• *Enough to fill and decorate one 8- to 9-inch cake* •

½ cup (2 to 3 large) eggs
½ cup (4 ounces) sugar
2 tablespoons (1 ounce) liqueur kirsch
1 cup (8 ounces) unsalted butter, at room temperature
¾ cup (3 ounces) finely chopped pistachio nuts, blanched if they are salted

In the top of a double boiler, over simmering, but not boiling, water, whisk the eggs and sugar until thick and the whisk marks keep their shape (125°F.). Remove from the heat and stir in the liqueur kirsch. Beat in the butter, chunk by chunk, until smooth; add the pistachio nuts. Chill until the desired spreading consistency is obtained.

## • ABOUT MERINGUE •

Meringue is a baked mixture of egg whites and sugar. It must be baked at a low temperature for a long time, 1 to 1½ hours, or placed in a 275°F. oven for 15 minutes and then left in the turned-off oven overnight. (Do not peek, as this would allow the heat to escape from the oven.) Meringue will keep 3 weeks if completely sealed away from air and moisture in a tin box. Meringue absorbs moisture and odors readily. Exercise extreme caution when handling meringue, as it is very brittle and will splinter or shatter at the slightest provocation. Cakes featuring meringue should be served immediately, as meringue gets soggy very quickly.

# *Meringue-Mousse Baskets*

A somewhat precious individual dessert, the baskets may be prepared in advance and filled just before serving.

• *10 servings* •

2 tablespoons (1 ounce) cocoa, packed
¾ cup sifted and then measured (3 ounces) confectioners' sugar
½ cup (about 4 large) egg whites
⅓ cup (2 ounces) granulated sugar

♠ ♠ ♠

2 cups Mousse au Chocolat, page 91
1 cup (8 ounces) whipping cream
1 tablespoon (½ ounce) granulated sugar
1 teaspoon liqueur kirsch (optional)

Preheat oven to 275°F.

Draw 10 circles, 3 inches in diameter, on a piece of wax paper 12 by 18 inches. Place the wax paper facedown on a 12-by-18-inch baking sheet. Butter and sprinkle it with granulated sugar.

Sift the cocoa and confectioners' sugar together twice; set aside. Beat the egg whites with 2 tablespoons of the granulated sugar until almost stiff. Add the remaining granulated sugar and beat until very stiff. Gently fold the cocoa mixture into the beaten egg whites. Place in a pastry bag fitted with a ½-inch nozzle tip and pipe disks within the circles drawn on the wax paper. To form the baskets, pipe a layer

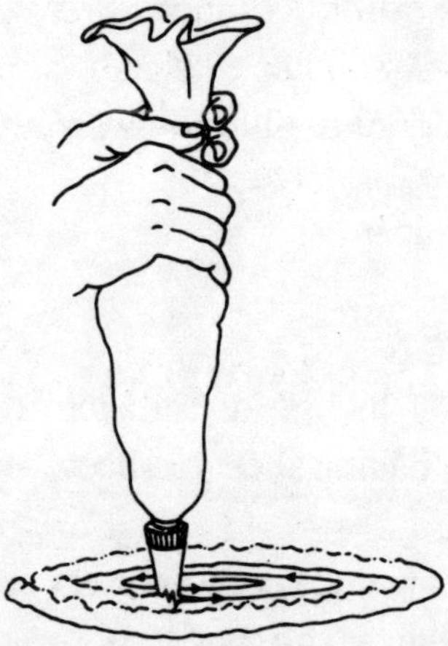

of meringue around the edge of each disk and then yet another layer on top of that. Bake until dry to the touch, about 1 to 1½ hours. Cool on the baking sheet and then peel off the wax paper.

Fill the baskets with the Mousse au Chocolat. Whip the cream with 1 tablespoon sugar and the liqueur kirsch, if desired. Put the whipped cream in a pastry bag fitted with a star tip and pipe over the mousse.

Serve immediately.

# Meringue-Mousse Torte

This torte looks particularly impressive.

• *8 to 10 servings* •

1/3 cup sifted and then measured (1 ounce) cocoa
1 1/4 cups sifted and then measured (5 ounces) confectioners' sugar
3/4 cup (5 to 6 large) egg whites
2/3 cup (5 1/2 ounces) granulated sugar
Mousse au Chocolat, page 91
Confectioners' sugar

Preheat oven to 275°F.

Draw three circles 7 inches in diameter on wax paper. Place the paper facedown on a baking sheet or sheets. Butter and sprinkle with granulated sugar.

Sift the cocoa and 1 1/4 cups confectioners' sugar together twice; set aside. Beat the egg whites with 2 tablespoons of the granulated sugar until almost stiff. Add the remaining granulated sugar and beat until very stiff. Fold the cocoa mixture into the beaten egg whites. Place in a pastry bag fitted with a 1/2-inch nozzle tip and pipe disks within the circles drawn on the wax paper. Pipe the remaining meringue into thin strips, about 1/4 inch wide and 3 inches long. Bake until dry to the touch, about 1 to 1 1/2 hours. Cool on the baking sheet and then peel off the wax paper.

Spread a fourth of the mousse over 1 disk; assemble another disk on top of it; spread another fourth of the mousse on top of it; assemble the remaining disk on the mousse; spread the remaining mousse over the top and sides of the assembled stack of disks. (Do not overwork the mousse or it will become runny.) Break up the thin strips of meringue into 1- to 1 1/2-inch pieces and press them over the surface of the mousse.

Serve immediately.

# *Vacherin au Chocolat*

A sophisticated ice cream cake made with a shell of meringue.

• *12 to 16 servings* •

1/4 cup (1 ounce) cocoa, packed
1 1/4 cups sifted and then measured (5 ounces) confectioners' sugar
2/3 cup (5 to 6 large) egg whites
5/8 cup (5 ounces) granulated sugar

♠ ♠ ♠

3 cups (1 1/2 pints) chocolate ice cream
1/2 cup (4 ounces) whipping cream
1 tablespoon (1/2 ounce) granulated sugar
1 tablespoon (1/2 ounce) liqueur kirsch (optional)
Chocolate Curls, page 69

Preheat oven to 325°F.

Draw 4 circles 8 inches in diameter on wax paper. Place the paper facedown on a baking sheet or sheets. Butter and sprinkle the paper with granulated sugar.

Sift the cocoa and confectioners' sugar together twice; set aside. Beat the egg whites with 1 tablespoon of the granulated sugar until almost stiff. Beat in the remaining granulated sugar until stiff. Gently fold the cocoa mixture into the beaten egg whites.

Place the meringue in a large pastry bag fitted with a 1/2-inch nozzle tip. Pipe an entire disk inside one of the circles drawn on the paper. Outline the remaining 3 circles and build another layer on top of each circle outline. Reserve about 1 cup of the meringue in a cool place or in the refrigerator. Bake the disk and the circles until somewhat dry, about 30 minutes. Cool and gently loosen the baked meringue from the paper. Dot the edges of the disk with the reserved unbaked meringue and place a baked meringue circle on top of it.

Dot the circle with unbaked meringue and place another circle on top of it. Repeat, using all the circles. Spread any remaining unbaked meringue on the outside of the shell with a palette knife. Make decorative borders on the sides and top of the shell with the pastry bag

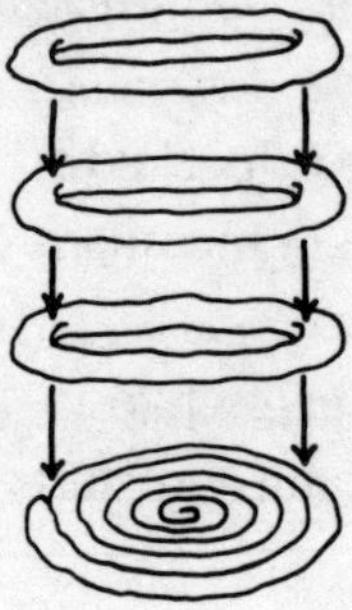

fitted with a star tip, if desired. Return to the oven and bake until very dry, about 30 minutes to 1 hour.

At serving time fill the shell with ice cream. Whip the cream with 1 tablespoon sugar and the liqueur kirsch, if desired. Place the whipped cream in a pastry bag fitted with a star tip and pipe a decorative border. Garnish with Chocolate Curls.

Serve immediately.

# *Honey Almond Cocoa Torte*

I developed this recipe for a friend who could eat no wheat or white sugar.

• *8 to 10 servings* •

¼ cup (1 ounce) cocoa, packed
1½ cups (6 ounces) finely ground unblanched almonds
4 large eggs, separated (½ cup whites, ⅓ cup yolks)
½ cup (6 ounces) honey
Chocolate Honey Buttercream, page 93

Preheat oven to 325°F.

Butter two 8-inch round pans, or any pans holding 4 cups of water each. Line them with wax paper, butter the paper, and flour the pans.

Sift the cocoa and fold it into the almonds; set aside. Beat the egg whites with 2 tablespoons of the honey until the peaks keep their shape; set aside. Beat the egg yolks with the remaining honey until thick and ribbonlike. Alternately, a third at a time, fold the beaten egg whites and the cocoa/almond mixture into the beaten egg yolks. Mix only until smooth. *Do not overmix.* Divide the batter equally between the prepared pans and bake until the cakes are slightly dry and start to shrink away from the sides of the pans, about 25 minutes. Cool 2 minutes in the pans, then gently invert onto a cooling rack. Decorate with Chocolate Honey Buttercream.

# CAKES WITH FRUIT OR JAM

# *Chocolate Apple Torte*

A dense torte made with grated apples, walnuts, chocolate, and almost no flour. The apples add a mild fruitiness. Allow a 12-hour setting time before decoration and a 30-minute setting time before serving.

• *12 to 16 servings* •

3 small apples
1½ cups (6 ounces) finely ground walnuts
¼ cup sifted and then measured (1 ounce) cake flour
2 ounces bittersweet chocolate
5 large eggs, separated (⅝ cup whites, ⅜ cup yolks)
¾ cup (6 ounces) sugar
2 to 3 tablespoons (1 to 1½ ounces) liqueur kirsch or
  Calvados (optional)
Chocolate Glaze, page 85

Preheat oven to 325°F.

Butter one 9-inch round pan, or any pan holding 6 cups of water. Line it with wax paper, butter the paper, and flour the pan.

Peel, core, and grate the apples; put them on a cloth towel. Squeeze the excess moisture from the apples; measure 1 cup. Blend the apples with the walnuts and flour; set aside. In the top of a double boiler, over hot, but not simmering, water, melt the chocolate; set aside. Beat the egg whites with ½ cup of the sugar until the peaks keep their shape; set aside. Beat the egg yolks with the remaining ¼ cup of sugar until thick and ribbonlike. Fold the chocolate into the beaten egg yolks. Alternately, a third at a time, fold the beaten egg whites and apple mixture into the chocolate mixture. Blend only until smooth. *Do not overmix.* Pour the batter into the prepared pan and bake until a knife inserted into the center of the torte comes out clean, about 1 hour. Loosen the springform and cool 10 minutes. Gently invert onto a piece of corrugated cardboard cut to the size of the torte and sprinkled with sugar.

Wrap securely with plastic and allow the torte to set at least 12 hours in the refrigerator before decorating. Then, sprinkle the torte with the liqueur kirsch or Calvados, if desired. Decorate with Chocolate Glaze.

# *Chocolate Apricot Cake*

Poached apricots fill this cake and are used as a garnish. The color contrast of the apricots with the chocolate is dramatically beautiful.

• *10 servings* •

1 cup (8 ounces) water
1 cup (8 ounces) sugar
Rind of 1 orange
1 pound slightly underripe apricots
1 Génoise au Chocolat, page 78, split into 2 layers; or 2 Cocoa-Almond Torte layers, page 154, or 2 Chocolate-Pistachio Torte layers, page 163
2 tablespoons (1 ounce) Grand Marnier
Chocolate Buttercream, page 82
1/4 cup (1 ounce) chopped pistachio nuts

In a heavy saucepan, bring to a boil the water, sugar, and orange rind. Turn the heat down to a simmer and cook 5 minutes. Wash, halve, and pit the apricots. Place them in the syrup, cover, and poach until soft, about 15 minutes. Remove the apricots from the syrup and cool them on a rack, allowing the excess moisture to drain.

*Black Hole Cake (page 183)*

*Bûche de Noël (page 184)*

*Chocolate Charlotte (page 186)*

*Doboshtorte (page 212)*

Sprinkle each layer of the cake or torte with 1 tablespoon Grand Marnier. Reserve 6 of the apricot halves. Coarsely chop the remaining apricots and place them between the layers of the cake. Decorate the top and sides of the cake with Chocolate Buttercream. Arrange the 6 apricot halves on top of the cake. Fill the wells of the apricots with the pistachio nuts.

# Chocolate Banana Cake

The bananas make this a very moist cake that keeps well.

• *10 to 12 servings* •

5 small bananas
2 tablespoons (1 ounce) milk
3 ounces bittersweet chocolate
3 large eggs, separated (1/3 cup whites, 1/4 cup yolks)
3/4 cup (6 ounces) sugar
1 cup sifted and then measured (4 ounces) cake flour
1 cup Crème Pâtissière (following recipe)
Confectioners' sugar

Preheat oven to 325°F.

Butter two 8-inch round pans, or any pans holding 4 cups of water each. Line them with wax paper, butter the paper, and flour the pans.

Place 2 bananas and the milk in an electric blender or food processor. Blend at low speed until homogenized; set aside. In the top of a double boiler, over hot, but not simmering, water, melt the chocolate; set aside. Beat the egg whites with 1/2 cup of the sugar until the peaks keep their shape; set aside. Beat the egg yolks with the remaining 1/4 cup sugar until thick and ribbonlike. Fold the bananas and the chocolate into the beaten egg yolks. Alternately, a third at a time, fold the beaten egg whites and the flour into the chocolate mixture. Mix only until smooth. *Do not overmix.* Divide the batter equally between the prepared pans and bake until a knife inserted into the center comes out clean, about 25 minutes. Cool 2 minutes in the pans, then gently invert onto a cooling rack.

When cool, split each layer into 2 layers. Spread Crème Pâtissière on 3 of the layers. Peel and cut 3 bananas into ⅛-inch segments. Place the banana slices on the crème. Assemble the cake with the crème and bananas between layers. Sprinkle the top with confectioners' sugar.

# Crème Pâtissière

A delicious, smooth, but not too sweet, version of the classic pastry cream. Make a charlotte with any leftovers.

• *2½ cups* •

2 cups (16 ounces) whipping cream
⅓ cup (2½ ounces) sugar
⅓ cup (about 4 to 5 large) egg yolks
3 tablespoons (1½ ounces) cornflour, packed
¼ cup (2 ounces) water
1-inch vanilla bean, or ¼ teaspoon vanilla extract

In the top of a double boiler, over simmering, but not boiling, water, place 1½ cups of the cream. Stir the sugar into the egg yolks and add the cornflour; set aside. Boil the water with the vanilla bean. Remove the bean, split it, and scrape out the inner flecks. (Do not discard the bean; when it is dry, add it to sugar to make vanilla sugar, page 11.) Add the water and the vanilla flecks or the vanilla extract to the egg yolk mixture and stir it into the warm cream. Cook, whisking constantly, until the mixture thickens and the whisk marks keep their shape (125°F.). Scrape the sides of the double boiler if the mixture seems to be sticking. Remove from the heat and stir in the remaining ½ cup cream to cool the mixture and stop the cooking. Place a piece of plastic wrap directly on top of the crème to prevent a skin from forming. Refrigerate until set, about 1 hour.

# *Crème Pâtissière au Chocolat*

Add ⅔ cup (2 ounces) grated bittersweet chocolate to the basic Crème Pâtissière (preceding recipe) mixture while it is cooking in the top of the double boiler.

# *Chocolate Blueberry Cake*

A festive-looking midsummer dessert. You can use bilberries instead of blueberries.

• *10 servings* •

1 Génoise au Chocolat, page 78, split into 2 layers, or 2 Cocoa-Almond Torte layers, page 154
3 tablespoons (1½ ounces) liqueur kirsch
1 basket (8 ounces) blueberries
1 cup (12 ounces) jelly (currant, blueberry, or raspberry)
2 cups (16 ounces) whipping cream
2 tablespoons (1 ounce) sugar

Sprinkle each layer of the cake or torte with 1 tablespoon liqueur kirsch. Wash and drain the blueberries. Simmer them in the jelly for 10 minutes. Strain away the excess jelly and cool the blueberries. Whip the cream with the sugar and 1 tablespoon liqueur kirsch. Mix half the prepared berries with ½ cup of the whipped cream. Spread this between the layers of the cake. Decorate the cake with the remaining whipped cream, arranging the remaining blueberries on top.

# *Chocolate Loganberry Cake*

A dense, moist cake with a hint of fruitiness. If you cannot obtain loganberries, use a mixture of raspberries and blackberries.

• *8 to 10 servings* •

4 ounces bittersweet chocolate
2 tablespoons (1 ounce) water or liqueur kirsch
2 tablespoons (1 ounce) loganberry preserves
3 large eggs, separated (⅓ cup whites, ¼ cup yolks)
⅔ cup (5½ ounces) sugar
1¼ cups sifted and then measured (5 ounces) cake flour

♠ ♠ ♠

¼ cup (2 ounces) liqueur kirsch (optional)
½ cup (4 ounces) loganberry preserves
Chocolate Loganberry Buttercream (following recipe)

Preheat oven to 325°F.

Butter one 8-inch round pan, or any pan holding 4 cups of water. Line it with wax paper, butter the paper, and flour the pan.

In the top of a double boiler, over hot, but not simmering, water, melt the chocolate with the water or liqueur kirsch. Stir in the 2 tablespoons loganberry preserves; set aside. Beat the egg whites with ⅓ cup of the sugar until the peaks keep their shape; set aside. Beat the egg yolks with the remaining ⅓ cup of sugar until thick and ribbon-like. Fold the chocolate into the beaten egg yolk. Alternately, a third at a time, fold the beaten egg whites and the flour into the chocolate mixture. Mix only until smooth. *Do not overmix.* Pour the batter into the prepared pan and bake until a knife inserted into the center of the cake comes out clean, about 30 minutes. Cool 2 minutes in the pan and then gently invert onto a cooling rack.

When cool, split the cake into 3 layers with a serrated knife. Sprinkle each layer with liqueur kirsch, if desired. Spread ½ cup loganberry preserves over the 3 layers and assemble the cake. Decorate with Chocolate Loganberry Buttercream.

# *Chocolate Loganberry Buttercream*

Loganberry preserves replace sugar in this recipe for buttercream, and impart an elusive flavor.

• *Enough to fill and decorate one 8- to 9-inch cake* •

5 ounces bittersweet chocolate
2 tablespoons (1 ounce) water or liqueur kirsch
½ cup (2 to 3 large) eggs
½ cup (6 ounces) loganberry preserves
1 cup (8 ounces) unsalted butter, at room temperature

In the top of a double boiler, over hot, but not simmering, water, melt the chocolate with the water or liqueur kirsch; set aside. In the top of a double boiler, over simmering, but not boiling, water, whisk the eggs and loganberry preserves until very thick and the whisk marks keep their shape (125°F.). Remove from the heat and fold in the chocolate. Beat in the butter, chunk by chunk, until very smooth. Chill until the desired spreading consistency is obtained.

# Chocolate Cranberry Cake

A spicy cranberry compote fills this special holiday cake.

• *10 servings* •

2 cups (16 ounces) cranberries
½ cup (4 ounces) water
1 cup (8 ounces) sugar
2-inch cinnamon stick or 2 teaspoons ground cinnamon
1 whole (¼ teaspoon ground) allspice
4 whole (¼ teaspoon ground) cloves
2 tablespoons Candied Citrus Rind, page 129 (optional)
2 tablespoons (1 ounce) Grand Marnier

♠ ♠ ♠

1 Génoise au Chocolat, split into 2 layers, page 78, or 2 Chocolate-Walnut Torte layers, page 164
2 tablespoons (1 ounce) Grand Marnier
Chocolate Buttercream, page 82

Wash the cranberries. Place them and the water in a heavy saucepan and bring to a boil. Turn the heat down to a simmer and cook for 1 hour. Add the sugar. Pulverize the spices and add to the cranberries with the Candied Citrus Rind if desired. Simmer for about 1 hour longer, or until very thick. Stir often when the mixture begins to thicken because it burns easily. Cool and add 2 tablespoons Grand Marnier.

Sprinkle each layer of the cake or torte with 1 tablespoon Grand Marnier. Spread the cranberry compote between the layers of the cake. Decorate with Chocolate Buttercream.

# *Cocoa Date Torte*

Very chewy, this torte is almost like candy. Dates stuffed with almonds are an attractive and easy garnish.

• *10 to 12 servings* •

1 cup (8 ounces) chopped and pitted dates
2/3 cup (3 ounces) cake crumbs, page 52
2 tablespoons (1/2 ounce) cocoa, packed
4 large eggs, separated (1/2 cup whites, 1/3 cup yolks)
1/2 cup (4 ounces) sugar
Chocolate Buttercream, page 82
12 whole pitted dates
12 whole blanched almonds

Preheat oven to 325°F.

Butter two 8-inch round pans, or any pans holding 4 cups of water each. Line them with wax paper, butter the paper, and flour the pans.

Mix the chopped dates with the crumbs and sift in the cocoa; set aside. Beat the egg whites with 1/4 cup of the sugar until the peaks keep their shape; set aside. Beat the egg yolks with the remaining 1/4 cup sugar until thick and ribbonlike. Alternately, a third at a time, fold the beaten egg whites and the date mixture into the beaten egg yolks. Mix only until smooth. *Do not overmix.* Pour the batter into the prepared pan and bake until a knife inserted into the center of the cakes comes out clean, about 20 to 25 minutes. Cool 2 minutes in the pans, then gently invert onto a cooling rack. Decorate with Chocolate Buttercream.

Stuff a blanched almond inside each of the whole dates. Arrange them on top of the torte.

# Dried Fruit and Brandy Chocolate Cake

A prosaic name belies the jewellike appearance of the marinated fruit within this cake. A 2-day marinating time is required before the cake is made.

• *10 to 12 servings* •

1 pound dried, pitted fruit: a mixture of prunes, dates, currants, apricots, pears, apples, and figs
1 cup (8 ounces) water
1 cup (8 ounces) sugar
1/3 cup (2 1/2 ounces) brandy

♠ ♠ ♠

6 ounces bittersweet chocolate
1/2 cup (4 ounces) unsalted butter
1/2 cup (6 ounces) chopped marinated dried fruit (about a quarter of the recipe above)
4 large eggs, separated (1/2 cup whites, 1/3 cup yolks)
1/2 cup (4 ounces) sugar
1 cup sifted and then measured (4 ounces) cake flour
1/4 cup brandy marinade (about half recipe above)
Chocolate Glaze, page 85

If the fruit was dried with sulfur or contains preservatives, pour boiling water over it and then drain. In a heavy saucepan, boil the water and 1 cup sugar. Turn the heat down to a simmer and cook for 5 minutes. Remove from the heat. When cool, add the brandy and fruit. Cover securely and allow to steep for at least 2 days. Drain off the marinade and reserve. Chop the fruit.

Preheat oven to 325°F.

Butter one 9-inch springform pan, or any pan holding 6 cups of water. Line it with wax paper, butter the paper, and flour the pan.

In the top of a double boiler, over hot, but not simmering, water, melt the chocolate and butter. Stir in the marinated fruit; set aside. Beat the egg whites with 1/4 cup of the sugar until peaks keep their shape; set aside. Beat the egg yolks with the remaining 1/4 cup of sugar until thick and ribbonlike. Fold the chocolate mixture into the beaten egg yolks. Alternately, a third at a time, fold the beaten egg whites and the flour into the chocolate mixture. Mix only until smooth. *Do not overmix.* Pour the batter into the prepared pan and bake until a knife inserted into the center of the cake comes out clean, about 25 minutes. Cool 2 minutes in the pan, loosen the springform and cool another 10 minutes, then gently invert onto a cooling rack.

When cool, split into 2 layers with a serrated knife. Sprinkle 2 tablespoons of the reserved brandy marinade on each layer. Spread the remaining dried fruit compote (about 12 ounces or 1 cup) between the layers of the cake, 1/3 cup between each layer. Decorate with Chocolate Glaze.

# *Four-Citrus Chocolate Cake*

The four citrus fruits provide a complex, enigmatic flavor complemented by chocolate.

• *10 to 12 servings* •

1 cup (4 to 5 large) eggs
2/3 cup Marmalade (following recipe) made with equal amounts oranges, lemons, grapefruit, and limes
1/4 cup (2 ounces) unsalted butter, melted
1 1/2 cups sifted and then measured (6 ounces) cake flour
1/4 cup (2 ounces) Grand Marnier
Citrus Chocolate Buttercream, page 127

Preheat oven to 325°F.

Butter two 8-inch round pans, or any pans holding 4 cups of water each. Line them with wax paper, butter the paper, and flour the pans.

Whisk the eggs and the marmalade in a mixing bowl set over simmering, but not boiling, water, until the mixture gets too hot to keep a finger in for more than a second (125°F.). Remove from the heat and beat with an electric mixer until very thick and creamy, about 5 to 10 minutes. Trickle in the butter while folding in the flour. Do this very quickly and efficiently. *Do not overmix.* Divide the batter equally between the prepared pans and bake until the sides of the cakes start to shrink away from the sides of the pans, about 20 minutes. Cool 2 minutes in the pans, then gently invert onto cooling racks.

Sprinkle each layer with 2 tablespoons Grand Marnier; decorate with Citrus Chocolate Buttercream.

# Marmalade

This recipe takes 3 days to prepare, but only an hour total working time. Very easy and inexpensive; use any kind and amount of citrus fruit, alone or in combination—preferably seedless and organically grown.

Citrus fruit
Water
Sugar

If organically grown fruit is unobtainable, soak the available fruit in hot salty water for an hour. Rinse well and rub dry. If you see white spots, these are undissolved wax; try to rub them off. If the fruit has a very thick white, inner layer (such as grapefruit) peel off the zest (the outer colored skin) with a potato peeler, reserve it, and discard the inner skin. Cut the fruit into very thin slices (⅛ inch thick). If the fruit peel does not have a thick inner skin (limes, oranges), simply slice the fruit, skin and all. (Be warned that citric acid in the fruit softens wooden cutting boards, making them very vulnerable to deep scratches if you are heavy-handed with your knife.) Discard the seeds and mix fruit slices with the zests. Measure and place in an enamel or stainless steel cooking pot. Measure an amount of water equal to the fruit. Boil the water and pour it over the fruit. Cover *immediately* and allow to sit undisturbed for 24 hours, unrefrigerated.

The next day, bring the mixture to a boil for 30 minutes, uncovered. Cover and allow to sit another 24 hours, unrefrigerated.

On the third day, measure the fruit and the water and add an equal amount of sugar. Bring to a boil, stirring constantly. Lower the heat and simmer, uncovered, for 1 to 2 hours, or until a spoonful "sets" on a plate after 5 minutes in the refrigerator. Skim off the foam. The fruit will be completely transparent and jewellike. Stir frequently during the last half hour to prevent the bottom from scorching. Pack the marmalade into sterilized jars and seal or simply refrigerate or freeze. If not completely sealed, the marmalade may crystallize in the refrigerator; it is still safe to use, however.

# Citrus Chocolate Buttercream

Also try this buttercream with Chocolate Banana Cake or Chocolate Apricot Cake.

• *Enough to fill and decorate one 8- to 9-inch cake* •

5 ounces bittersweet chocolate
2 tablespoons (1 ounce) Grand Marnier
½ cup (2 to 3 large) eggs
½ cup (6 ounces) Marmalade (preceding recipe)
1 cup (8 ounces) unsalted butter, at room temperature

In the top of a double boiler, over hot, but not simmering, water, melt the chocolate and Grand Marnier; set aside. In the top of a double boiler, over simmering, but not boiling, water, whisk the eggs and marmalade until thick and the whisk marks keep their shape (125°F.). Remove from the heat and fold in the chocolate. Beat in the butter, chunk by chunk, until smooth. Chill until the desired spreading consistency is obtained.

# *Chocolate Jewel Cake*

Hidden gems of chocolate, nuts, Candied Citrus Rind, raisins, and angelica nestle in this confection. Without the buttercream, but sprinkled with confectioners' sugar, take this cake as a special dessert on a picnic.

• *10 to 12 servings* •

2 ounces bittersweet chocolate, grated (2/3 cup)
1/2 cup (2 ounces) chopped walnuts or almonds
1/4 cup (2 ounces) Candied Citrus Rind (following recipe)
1/4 cup (2 ounces) chopped raisins or currants
1-inch candied angelica root (optional)
4 large eggs, separated (1/2 cup whites, 1/3 cup yolks)
1/2 cup (4 ounces) sugar
2 to 4 tablespoons (1 to 2 ounces) liqueur kirsch
Chocolate Buttercream, page 82

Preheat oven to 325°F.

Butter two 8-inch round pans, or any pans holding 4 cups of water each. Line them with wax paper, butter the paper, and flour the pans.

Mix together the chocolate, nuts, Candied Citrus Rind, raisins or currants and angelica root; set aside. Beat the egg whites with 1/4 cup of the sugar until the peaks keep their shape; set aside. Beat the egg yolks with the remaining ¼ cup sugar until thick and ribbonlike. Alternately, a third at a time, fold the beaten egg whites and the chocolate mixture into the beaten egg yolks. Mix only until smooth. *Do not overmix.* Divide the batter equally between the prepared pans and bake until a knife inserted into the center of the cakes comes out clean, about 20 to 25 minutes. Cool 2 minutes in the pan, then gently invert onto a cooling rack.

Sprinkle each layer with 1 or 2 tablespoons liqueur kirsch. Decorate with Chocolate Buttercream.

# *Candied Citrus Rind*

A wonderful garnish for cakes, these dainties sparkle against a background of rich chocolate.

Citrus fruit
Water
Sugar

If organically grown fruit is unobtainable, soak the available fruit in hot, salty water for an hour. Rinse well and rub dry. Try to rub off any remaining white spots (undissolved wax). Peel off the rind, leaving as little of the white inner skin as possible. Cut the rind into squares, hearts, diamonds, or other fanciful shapes. Put the rinds in a stainless steel or enamel saucepan and cover them with cold water.

Bring to a boil, then drain off the water. Repeat this procedure three times for a total of four times. For each cup of rinds, make a sugar syrup using 1/4 cup water to 1/2 cup sugar. Boil the water and sugar for 5 minutes, then add the rinds. Cook until the rinds have absorbed all the syrup, about 1 hour. Spread them out on a baking sheet lined with wax paper. Set away from pests and allow to dry, unrefrigerated, 4 to 5 days. When completely dry, store in an uncovered container away from moisture and light.

# *Lemon and Chocolate Cake*

Especially moist and rich, this cake is based on a hollandaise sauce, the same kind one would put on asparagus. When you have extra egg yolks, make this cake.

• *10 to 12 servings* •

1/4 cup (about 3 large) egg yolks
1 tablespoon (1/2 ounce) lemon juice
1/2 cup (4 ounces) unsalted butter, melted and still hot

♠ ♠ ♠

3 ounces unsweetened chocolate
3 large eggs, separated (1/3 cup whites, 1/4 cup yolks)
1 cup (8 ounces) sugar
1 cup sifted and then measured (4 ounces) cake flour

♠ ♠ ♠

Lemon Custard Filling (following recipe)
Chocolate Buttercream, page 82
Candied Citrus Rind (preceding recipe)

Preheat oven to 325°F.

Butter two 8-inch round pans, or any pans holding 4 cups of water each. Line them with wax paper, butter the paper, and flour the pans.

To make the hollandaise, place ¼ cup egg yolks and the lemon juice in an electric blender. Blend at low speed for 30 seconds. With the motor still running, slowly pour in the melted butter. Continue blending about 1 minute or until thick; set aside.

In the top of a double boiler, over hot, but not simmering, water, melt the chocolate; set aside. Beat the egg whites with ½ cup of the sugar until the peaks keep their shape; set aside. Beat ¼ cup egg yolks with the remaining ½ cup sugar until thick and ribbonlike. Fold the hollandaise and chocolate into the beaten egg yolks. Alternately, a third at a time, fold the beaten egg whites and flour into the chocolate mixture. Mix only until smooth. *Do not overmix.* Divide the batter equally between the prepared pans and bake until a knife inserted into the center of the cake comes out clean, about 25 minutes. Cool 2 minutes in the pan, then gently invert onto a cooling rack.

When cool, split each layer in 2 with a serrated knife. Spread Lemon Custard Filling between the layers and decorate with Chocolate Buttercream. Garnish with Candied Citrus Rind.

# *Lemon Custard Filling*

This filling is delicious with Chocolate Loganberry Cake or Pavlova.

• *Enough to fill one 8- to 9-inch four-layer cake* •

1 tablespoon (¼ ounce) cornflour
½ cup (4 ounces) sugar
⅓ cup (about 4 to 5 large) egg yolks
1 tablespoon (½ ounce) unsalted butter, at room temperature
1 lemon rind, grated
Juice of 2 lemons
Water

Sift the cornflour and the sugar together into the egg yolks. Add the butter and beat until smooth. Grate the lemon rind into a measuring cup; juice the lemons into the same measuring cup; add enough water to make ½ cup liquid. Pour the liquid mixture into the egg yolk mixture and mix well. Place in the top of a double boiler, over simmering, but not boiling, water, and cook, whisking constantly until the custard is thick and the whisk marks keep their shape (125°F.). Remove from the heat and continue whisking until cool. This filling may be made in advance and stored refrigerated up to a week.

# *Chocolate Nectarine Cake*

Poached nectarines are a refreshingly light contrast to the richness of chocolate.

• *10 servings* •

1 cup (8 ounces) water
1 cup (8 ounces) sugar
2 tablespoons (1 ounce) brandy
2 large (16 ounces) underripe nectarines

♠ ♠ ♠

1 Génoise au Chocolat, split into 2 layers, page 78, or
 2 Chocolate-Walnut Torte layers, page 164
2 tablespoons (1 ounce) brandy
¼ cup Crème Pâtissière (optional), page 118
Chocolate Buttercream, page 82

In a heavy saucepan, boil the water and sugar. Turn the heat down to a simmer and cook 5 minutes. Add 2 tablespoons brandy. Wash, halve, pit, but do not peel the nectarines. Cover them with the syrup and poach until soft but still sliceable, about 15 to 20 minutes. Remove the fruit from the syrup and cool on a rack, allowing the excess moisture to drain off. When thoroughly cooled, gently rub off the skins. Slice into ⅛-inch segments.

Sprinkle each layer of the cake or torte with 1 tablespoon brandy. Spread Crème Pâtissière on 1 layer of the cake, if desired. Place the slices from 1 nectarine on the crème or on the cake, and assemble the other layer on top of them. Decorate with Chocolate Buttercream. Arrange the remaining nectarine slices on top of the cake (see photograph).

# *Orange and Chocolate Cake*

Orange is a natural complement to chocolate, and this is a memorable creation. A 2-hour setting time is required before serving.

• *10 servings* •

1 Génoise Simple, page 78
2 tablespoons (1 ounce) Grand Marnier
1 cup Mousse au Chocolat, page 91
¼ cup (4 ounces) Marmalade, page 126, made exclusively with oranges
Chocolate Glaze, page 85
Candied Citrus Rind, page 129, made preferably with oranges

Split the génoise into 2 layers with a serrated knife. Sprinkle each layer with 1 tablespoon Grand Marnier. Spread mousse on 1 layer and spread the marmalade over the mousse. Place the remaining layer on the marmalade. Decorate with Chocolate Glaze and garnish with Candied Citrus Rind.

# *Pavlova*

A chocolate kiwi cake. Kiwi fruit was a favorite of the ballerina Anna Pavlova.

• *10 servings* •

1 Génoise au Chocolat, page 78, split into 2 layers
¼ cup plus 1 teaspoon (about 2 ounces) Grand Marnier
4 kiwi fruit
½ cup Crème Pâtissière, page 118
1½ cups (12 ounces) whipping cream
1 tablespoon (½ ounce) sugar

Sprinkle each layer of the génoise with 2 tablespoons Grand Marnier. Peel and slice the kiwi fruit into ⅛-inch slices. Spread the crème on 1 layer of the cake and place 2 sliced kiwis on it. Place the second layer on the kiwis. Whip the cream with the sugar and 1 teaspoon Grand Marnier. Decorate the cake with the whipped cream and garnish with the remaining kiwi slices (see photograph).

# *Chocolate Peach Cake*

Peaches and cream and a touch of port make this a fanciful dessert for a special occasion.

• *8 to 10 servings* •

2 large (16 ounces) underripe peaches
1 cup (8 ounces) port
1 cup (8 ounces) water

♠ ♠ ♠

1 Génoise au Chocolat, page 78, split into 2 layers
½ cup Crème Pâtissière, page 118
Chocolate and Port Buttercream (following recipe)

Wash, halve, and pit, but do not peel, the peaches. In a heavy saucepan, place the port, water, and peaches. Cover and poach until soft but still sliceable, about 15 to 20 minutes. Remove the fruit from the syrup and cook on a rack, allowing the excess moisture to drain off. When thoroughly cooled, gently rub off the skins. Slice into ⅛-inch slices.

Spread the Crème Pâtissière on 1 of the layers. Place the slices from 1 peach on the crème and assemble the other layer on top of them. Decorate with Chocolate and Port Buttercream.

# *Chocolate and Port Buttercream*

Chocolate and port are an unusual, but superb, combination.

• *Enough to fill and decorate one 8- to 9-inch cake* •

5 ounces bittersweet chocolate
¼ cup (2 ounces) port
½ cup (2 to 3 large) eggs
⅓ cup (2½ ounces) sugar
1 cup (8 ounces) unsalted butter, at room temperature

In the top of a double boiler, over hot, but not simmering, water, melt the chocolate with the port; set aside. In the top of a double boiler, over simmering, but not boiling, water, whisk the eggs and sugar until thick and the whisk marks keep their shape (125°F.). Remove from the heat and fold in the chocolate. Beat in the butter, chunk by chunk, until smooth. Chill until the desired spreading consistency is obtained.

# *Chocolate Spiced-Pear Cake*

A sophisticated cake that is as beautiful as it is delicious.

• *10 servings* •

2 cups (16 ounces) water
1 cup (8 ounces) sugar
2-inch cinnamon stick or 1 teaspoon ground cinnamon
6 whole (or ½ teaspoon ground) cloves
¼ cup (2 ounces) brandy
2 large (16 ounces) underripe Anjou pears

♠ ♠ ♠

1 Génoise au Chocolat, page 78, split into 2 layers
¼ cup Crème Pâtissière, page 118
Chocolate Buttercream, page 82

In a heavy saucepan, boil the water, sugar, cinnamon, and cloves 1 minute. Turn the heat down to a simmer and cook 5 minutes. Peel, core, and halve the pears. Add them to the syrup, cover, and poach until soft but still sliceable, about 20 minutes. Remove the fruit from the syrup and cool on a rack, allowing the excess moisture to drain off. Slice into ⅛-inch slices across the width.

Spread the Crème Pâtissière on 1 of the layers. Place the slices from

1 of the pears on the crème and assemble the other layer on top of them. Decorate with Chocolate Buttercream. Arrange the remaining pear slices on top of the cake in a rose pattern (see the photograph of the Chocolate Burgundy Pear Cake).

# *Chocolate Burgundy-Pear Cake*

Pears poached in wine are wonderful by themselves. They are even more wonderful as part of this magnificent cake.

• *10 servings* •

1 cup (8 ounces) sugar
2 cups (16 ounces) Burgundy
2-inch vanilla bean (optional)
2 large (16 ounces) underripe Anjou pears

♠ ♠ ♠

1 Génoise Simple, page 78, split into 2 layers
¼ cup Crème Pâtissière, page 118, or Crème Pâtissière au Chocolat, page 119
Chocolate Glaze, page 85
¼ cup (1 ounce) chopped pistachio nuts

In a heavy saucepan, dissolve the sugar in the wine. Add the vanilla bean, if desired. Peel, core, and halve the pears. Poach, covered, until soft but still sliceable, about 20 minutes. Remove the fruit from the poaching liquid and cool on a rack, allowing the excess moisture to drain off. Slice into ⅛-inch segments across the width.

Spread the Crème Pâtissière on 1 layer of the génoise. Place the slices from 1 pear on the crème and assemble the other layer on top of them. Decorate with Chocolate Glaze. Arrange the remaining pear slices on top of the cake in a rose pattern (see photograph). Press the pistachio nuts into the sides of the cake.

# *Pineapple Chocolate Cake*

Golden nuggets of pineapple garnish this cake inside and out.

• *8 to 10 servings* •

1 Génoise au Chocolat, split into 2 layers, page 78
3 tablespoons (1½ ounces) liqueur kirsch
¼ cup Crème Pâtissière, page 118
2 cups drained fresh pineapple segments
2 cups (16 ounces) whipping cream
1 tablespoon (½ ounce) sugar
½ cup (2 ounces) chopped pistachio nuts (optional)
Chocolate Curls (optional), page 69

Sprinkle each layer of the génoise with 1 tablespoon liqueur kirsch Spread the Crème Pâtissière on 1 layer of the cake and press 1 cup of the pineapple segments into it. Whip the cream with 1 tablespoon liqueur kirsch and the sugar. Assemble the cake and decorate with whipped cream. Arrange the remaining 1 cup pineapple segments on top of the cake and garnish with the pistachio nuts and Chocolate Curls if desired.

# Pomegranate Chocolate Cake

Some scholars claim that the Forbidden Fruit in the Garden of Eden was the pomegranate, not an apple. Perhaps this cake should be known as true "Devil's Food."

• *10 to 12 servings* •

1 Dense, Moist Chocolate Cake, page 81, split into 2 layers
1/4 cup (2 ounces) liqueur kirsch
1/2 cup (6 ounces) Pomegranate Jelly (following recipe)
Pomegranate Buttercream, page 140

Sprinkle each layer of the cake with 2 tablespoons liqueur kirsch. Spread the Pomegranate Jelly between the layers and decorate with Pomegranate Buttercream.

# Pomegranate Jelly

Very easy and exotic-tasting.

• *About 2 cups* •

5 large pomegranates (1 1/4 pounds)
Water
Sugar
Juice of 1 lemon

Wash the pomegranates. Cut off the pips, quarter the fruit, and place it in a stainless steel or enamel saucepan. Add just enough water to cover. Bring to a boil. Lower the heat and simmer for 1 hour. Strain through a jelly bag, being careful not to crush any of the seeds—they will impart a *very* bitter taste. Measure this juice and add an equal amount of sugar. Bring to a boil, stirring constantly. Lower the heat and simmer for about 1 hour longer, or until very thick and a spoonful "sets" on a plate after 5 minutes in the refrigerator. Skim off the foam and discard. Pack the jelly in sterilized jars and seal, or simply refrigerate or freeze.

# *Pomegranate Buttercream*

This buttercream is a lovely light raspberry color.

• *Enough to fill and decorate one 8- to 9-inch cake* •

½ cup (2 to 3 large) eggs
⅓ cup (4 ounces) Pomegranate Jelly (preceding recipe)
2 tablespoons (1 ounce) liqueur kirsch
1 cup (8 ounces) unsalted butter, at room temperature

In the top of a double boiler, over simmering, but not boiling, water, whisk the eggs and jelly until thick and the whisk marks keep their shape (125°F.). Remove from the heat and whisk in the liqueur kirsch. Beat in the butter, chunk by chunk, until smooth. Chill until the desired spreading consistency is obtained.

# Chocolate Prune Torte

Not an incongruous combination at all, the prunes taste almost like raisins with chocolate, but are fruitier and more flavorful.

• *10 to 12 servings* •

- 1/4 cup (2 ounces) chopped pitted prunes
- 1/2 cup (2 ounces) finely ground almonds
- 1/2 cup (2 ounces) cake crumbs
- 1/3 cup bittersweet chocolate, grated (1 ounce)
- 4 large eggs, separated (1/2 cup whites, 1/3 cup yolks)
- 1/2 cup (4 ounces) sugar
- 2 tablespoons (1 ounce) liqueur kirsch
- Chocolate Buttercream, page 82, or Chocolate Glaze, page 85

Preheat oven to 325°F.

Butter two 8-inch round pans, or any pans holding 4 cups of water each. Line them with wax paper, butter the paper, and flour the pans.

Mix together the prunes, almonds, cake crumbs, and chocolate; set aside. Beat the egg whites with 1/4 cup of the sugar until the peaks keep their shape; set aside. Beat the egg yolks with the remaining 1/4 cup sugar until thick and ribbonlike. Alternately, a third at a time, fold the beaten egg whites and the prune mixture into the beaten egg yolks. Mix only until smooth. *Do not overmix.* Divide the batter equally between the 2 prepared pans and bake until the layers start to shrink away from the sides of the pan, about 25 minutes. Cool 2 minutes in the pans, then gently invert onto a cooling rack. Sprinkle each layer with 1 tablespoon liqueur kirsch. Decorate with Chocolate Buttercream or Chocolate Glaze.

# Chocolate and Spiced-Prune Cake

Spiced prune compote contrasts with a honey cake for an Old World taste.

• *10 to 12 servings* •

1 cup (8 ounces) chopped pitted prunes
1 cup (8 ounces) water
1 tablespoon grated orange rind
2-inch cinnamon stick, freshly ground (or 1 teaspoon ground cinnamon)
6 whole cloves, freshly ground (or ½ teaspoon ground)
2 whole allspice, freshly ground (or ¼ teaspoon ground)

♠ ♠ ♠

1 Honey Chocolate Cake, page 92, split into 2 layers
2 tablespoons (1 ounce) Grand Marnier
Chocolate Glaze, page 85

In a heavy saucepan, place the prunes, water, orange rind, and spices. Simmer for 15 minutes, stirring occasionally.

Sprinkle each layer of the cake with 1 tablespoon Grand Marnier, Spread the cooked prune mixture between the layers and assemble the cake. Decorate with Chocolate Glaze.

# Chocolate Quince Cake

A very moist cake made with homemade quince butter, nuts, and cocoa.

• *8 to 10 servings* •

2 cups (8 ounces) finely ground unblanched almonds
2 tablespoons (1/2 ounce) cocoa, packed
5 large eggs, separated (5/8 cup whites, 3/8 cup yolks)
1 cup plus 1 tablespoon (about 8 ounces) sugar
1 1/2 cups (18 ounces) Quince Butter (following recipe)
1 cup (8 ounces) whipping cream
1 tablespoon Grand Marnier (optional)

Preheat oven to 325°F.

Butter and flour a tube pan holding 8 cups of water.

Sift the almonds and the cocoa together twice; set aside. Beat the egg whites with 1/2 cup of the sugar until the peaks keep their shape; set aside. Beat the egg yolks with 1/2 cup sugar until thick and ribbon-like. Fold 1/2 cup Quince Butter into the beaten egg yolks. Alternately, a third at a time, fold the beaten egg whites and the almond mixture into the egg yolks. Mix only until smooth. *Do not overmix.* Pour the batter into the prepared pan and bake until a knife inserted into the center of the cake comes out clean and the cake starts to shrink away from the sides of the pan, about 1 to 1 1/2 hours. Cool 10 minutes in the pan, then gently invert onto a cooling rack. Place the cake on the serving platter and put the remaining cup of Quince Butter in the center well. Whip the cream with 1 tablespoon of sugar and the Grand Marnier. Place the whipped cream in a pastry bag fitted with a star tip and pipe a decorative design on the cake.

# *Quince Butter*

Similar to apple butter, but with a more interesting and unusual flavor. Jelly bags are available in cookware stores, or use an old nylon stocking.

• *2 cups* •

3 large quinces ($1\frac{1}{2}$ pounds)
Sugar
Juice of 1 lemon
Water

Wash the quinces and rub the fuzz off the skin. Core them and put the seeds and pips in a jelly bag. Cut the quinces into small cubes and measure by packing them tightly into a measuring cup or by weight. Measure an equal amount of sugar. Place the fruit in a heavy stainless steel or enamel saucepan and cover with water. Add the sugar, lemon juice, and jelly bag containing the seeds. Bring to a boil. Lower the heat and simmer, uncovered, for 1 to $1\frac{1}{2}$ hours, or until the pulp is very soft and the liquid turns bright red. Skim off the foam. Remove the jelly bag and discard the seeds. Put the fruit through a food mill or press through a strainer and discard the skins. Pack into sterilized jars and seal, or simply refrigerate or freeze.

# Cocoa Raisin Torte

A chewy moist torte made with raisins, cake crumbs, and cocoa.

• *10 to 12 servings* •

1 cup (6 ounces) chopped raisins
$\frac{1}{2}$ cup (2 ounces) cake crumbs
2 tablespoons ($\frac{1}{2}$ ounce) cocoa, packed
4 large eggs, separated ($\frac{1}{2}$ cup whites, $\frac{1}{3}$ cup yolks)
$\frac{2}{3}$ cup ($5\frac{1}{2}$ ounces) sugar
2 tablespoons (1 ounce) liqueur kirsch (optional)
Chocolate Buttercream, page 82

Preheat oven to 325°F.

Butter two 8-inch round pans, or any pans holding 4 cups of water each. Line them with wax paper, butter the paper, and flour the pans.

Mix the raisins and cake crumbs and sift the cocoa into them; set aside. Beat the egg whites with half of the sugar until the peaks keep their shape; set aside. Beat the egg yolks with the remaining sugar until thick and ribbonlike. Alternately, a third at a time, fold the beaten egg whites and the raisin mixture into the beaten egg yolks. Mix only until smooth. *Do not overmix.* Divide the batter equally between the prepared pans and bake until a knife inserted into the center of the cakes comes out clean, about 20 to 25 minutes. Cool 2 minutes in the pan, then gently invert onto a cooling rack. Sprinkle each layer with 1 tablespoon liqueur kirsch, if desired, and decorate with Chocolate Buttercream.

# *Chocolate Raspberry Torte*

Raspberries and whipped cream are a dramatic and beautiful color contrast. This torte looks almost too good to cut into, but it is equally good to eat.

• *10 servings* •

1 Génoise au Chocolat, split into 2 layers, page 78, or 2 Cocoa-Hazelnut Torte layers, page 158
4 to 6 tablespoons (2 to 3 ounces) liqueur kirsch
2 cups (16 ounces) whipping cream
2 tablespoons (1 ounce) sugar
2 baskets (8 ounces) raspberries

Sprinkle each layer of the cake or torte with 1 to 2 tablespoons liqueur kirsch. Whip the cream with the sugar and 1 tablespoon liqueur kirsch. Do not wash the raspberries unless they seem dusty. Separate the more-perfect from the less-perfect berries to get an equal amount of each. Marinate the less-perfect berries in 1 tablespoon liqueur kirsch for 5 minutes. Mix the marinated berries with ½ cup of the whipped cream. Taste and adjust the sugar if necessary, then spread it between the layers. Decorate the cake with the remaining whipped cream. Garnish with the remaining berries (see photograph).

# *Schwartzwälder*

Black Forest Cake is widely available commercially but is usually disappointing. This version will *not* disappoint, with its brandied cherries, chocolate sponge cake, chocolate cream, whipped cream, and Chocolate Curls. At least 3 days are required for the cherries to steep in the brandy.

• *8 to 10 servings* •

½ cup (4 ounces) brandy
½ cup (8 ounces) packed morello cherries, pitted

♠ ♠ ♠

1 cup sifted and then measured (4 ounces) cake flour
¼ cup (1 ounce) cocoa, packed
¾ cup (3 to 4 large) eggs
½ cup (4 ounces) sugar
2 tablespoons (1 ounce) unsalted butter, melted

♠ ♠ ♠

4 to 7 tablespoons reserved brandy marinade
2 cups (16 ounces) whipping cream
¼ cup (2 ounces) sugar
2 ounces bittersweet chocolate
Chocolate Curls, page 69

Pour the brandy over the cherries. Cover and steep for at least 3 days.

Preheat oven to 325°F.

Butter one 8-inch round pan, or any pan holding 4 cups of water. Line it with wax paper, butter the paper, and flour the pan.

Sift the flour and cocoa together twice; set aside. In a heavy mixing bowl, over hot but not boiling water, whisk the eggs and ½ cup sugar until the mixture is too hot to keep a finger in for more than a second (125°F.). Remove from the heat and beat with an electric mixer until very thick and creamy, about 10 minutes. Alternately fold in the flour/cocoa mixture and trickle the butter into the beaten eggs. Mix only until smooth. *Do not overmix.* Pour the batter into the prepared pan and bake until a knife inserted into the center of the cake comes out clean, about 20 to 25 minutes. Cool 2 minutes in the pan, then gently invert onto a cooling rack. When cool, split the cake into 3 layers with a serrated knife.

Drain the marinade off the cherries and reserve it. Sprinkle each of the 3 layers with 1 to 2 tablespoons of the marinade.

Whip the cream with ¼ cup sugar and 1 tablespoon of reserved brandy marinade. In the top of a double boiler, over hot, but not simmering, water, melt the chocolate; cool slightly. Fold ½ cup of the whipped cream into the chocolate and spread over the bottom layer of the cake. Place the middle layer on the chocolate cream and spread ½ cup of the plain whipped cream over it. Press the cherries into the whipped cream and place the top layer on the cherries. Spread the remaining whipped cream over the top and sides of the cake. Garnish with Chocolate Curls.

## *Morello Cherry Chocolate Cake*

A cake for chocolate-covered-cherry lovers. At least 3 days is required for the cherries to steep in the brandy.

• *10 to 12 servings* •

About 1 cup (8 ounces) brandy
1½ cups (1 pound) packed morello cherries, pitted

♠ ♠ ♠

6 ounces bittersweet chocolate
½ cup (4 ounces) unsalted butter
4 large eggs, separated (½ cup whites, ⅓ cup yolks)
⅔ cup (5½ ounces) sugar
1 cup sifted and then measured (4 ounces) cake flour
Marinated cherries (recipe above), chopped
Chocolate Glaze, page 85

Pour the brandy over the cherries to cover. Cover and steep for at least 3 days.

Preheat oven to 325°F.

Butter one 9-inch round pan, or any pan holding 6 cups of water. Line it with wax paper, butter the paper, and flour the pan.

Drain the brandy off the cherries and reserve. Measure ½ cup of cherries. Set aside the remaining cherries.

In the top of a double boiler, over hot, but not simmering, water, melt the chocolate and butter. Stir in the ½ cup cherries and 2 tablespoons of the brandy marinade. Beat the egg whites with ½ cup of the sugar until the peaks keep their shape; set aside. Beat the egg yolks with the remaining sugar until thick and ribbonlike. Fold the chocolate mixture into the beaten egg yolks. Alternately, a third at a time, fold the beaten egg whites and the flour into the chocolate mixture. Mix only until smooth. *Do not overmix.* Pour the batter into the prepared pan and bake until a knife inserted into the center of the cake comes out clean, about 25 minutes. Cool 2 minutes in the pan, then gently invert onto a cooling rack.

When cooled, split the cake into 2 layers with a serrated knife. Sprinkle each layer with 2 tablespoons of the reserved brandy mari-

*Bourbon and Pecan Chocolate Cake (page 169) with Chocolate Glaze (page 85); Torta Sorentina (page 220) with Chocolate Glaze (page 85)*

*Pain au Chocolat (top) (page 222); Chocolate and Three Nut Coffeecake (page 224)*

nade. Assemble the cake with the remaining brandied cherries between the layers. Decorate with Chocolate Glaze.

# *Chocolate Strawberry Cake*

Beautiful, impressive, and easy.

• *10 servings* •

1 Génoise au Chocolat, split into 2 layers, page 78, or 2 Cocoa-Almond Torte layers, page 154
5 to 7 tablespoons (2½ to 3½ ounces) liqueur kirsch
2 cups (16 ounces) whipping cream
2 tablespoons (1 ounce) sugar
Two 4-ounce baskets strawberries
Chocolate Curls (optional), page 69

Sprinkle each layer of the cake or torte with 1 to 2 tablespoons liqueur kirsch. Whip the cream with the sugar and 2 tablespoons liqueur kirsch. Wash and remove the stems from the strawberries. Separate the more-perfect from the less-perfect berries to get an equal amount of each. Slice the less-perfect berries and marinate them in 1 tablespoon liqueur kirsch for 5 minutes. Mix the marinated berries with ½ cup of the whipped cream. Taste it and adjust the sugar if necessary, then spread it between the layers. Decorate the cake with the remaining whipped cream. Garnish with the remaining berries and Chocolate Curls, if desired.

# CAKES WITH NUTS

# *Chocolate-Almond Torte with Citrus and Spice*

A moist and flavorful confection that is especially appropriate for Thanksgiving or Christmas.

• *12 to 16 servings* •

2 whole or 1 big pinch ground cloves
1 whole or 1 big pinch ground allspice
1-inch cinnamon stick or 1/4 teaspoon ground cinnamon
1 lemon rind, grated
2 ounces bittersweet chocolate, grated (2/3 cup)
1 1/2 cups (6 ounces) finely ground unblanched almonds
4 large eggs, separated (1/2 cup whites, 1/3 cup yolks)
1/2 cup (4 ounces) sugar
2 to 4 tablespoons (1 to 2 ounces) liqueur kirsch
Chocolate Glaze, page 85

Preheat oven to 325°F.

Butter one 9-inch round springform pan, or any pan holding 6 cups of water. Line it with wax paper, butter the paper, and flour the pan.

Pulverize the whole spices and mix with the lemon rind, grated chocolate, and almonds; set aside. Beat the egg whites with 1/4 cup of the sugar until the peaks keep their shape; set aside. Beat the egg yolks with the remaining 1/4 cup sugar until thick and ribbonlike. Alternately, a third at a time, fold the beaten egg whites and the almond mixture into the beaten egg yolks. Mix only until smooth. *Do not overmix.* Pour the batter into the prepared pan and bake until a knife inserted into the center of the torte comes out clean, about 35 to 40 minutes. Loosen the springform and cool 10 minutes, then gently invert onto a cooling rack. Sprinkle the liqueur kirsch on the torte and decorate with Chocolate Glaze.

# *Cocoa-Almond Torte*

A dessert that manages to be both light and rich simultaneously.

• *8 to 10 servings* •

2 tablespoons (1/2 ounce) cocoa, packed
3/4 cup (3 ounces) finely ground unblanched almonds
4 large eggs, separated (1/2 cup whites, 1/3 cup yolks)
2/3 cup (5 1/2 ounces) sugar
2 tablespoons (1 ounce) kirsch or other liqueur
Chocolate-Almond Buttercream (following recipe)
12 whole unblanched almonds

Preheat oven to 325°F.

Butter two 8-inch round pans, or any pans holding 4 cups of water each. Line them with wax paper, butter the paper, and flour the pan.

Sift the cocoa into the ground almonds; set aside. Beat the egg whites with 1/2 cup of the sugar until the peaks keep their shape; set aside. Beat the egg yolks with the remaining sugar until thick and ribbonlike. Alternately, a third at a time, fold the beaten egg whites and the almond mixture into the beaten egg yolks. Mix only until smooth. *Do not overmix.* Divide the batter equally between the prepared pans and bake until the layers are dry and start to shrink away from the sides of the pans, about 35 minutes. Cool 2 minutes in the pans, then gently invert onto a cooling rack. When cooled, sprinkle with liqueur and decorate with Chocolate-Almond Buttercream. Garnish by placing the 12 whole almonds on top of the torte.

# Chocolate-Almond Buttercream

Almost like a chocolate marzipan.

• *Enough to fill and decorate one 8- to 9-inch cake* •

3 ounces bittersweet chocolate
2 tablespoons (1 ounce) coffee or liqueur
½ cup (2 to 3 large) eggs
½ cup (4 ounces) sugar
½ cup (2 ounces) very finely ground blanched almonds
1 cup (8 ounces) unsalted butter, very soft

In the top of a double boiler, over hot, but not simmering, water, melt the chocolate with the coffee or liqueur; set aside. In the top of a double boiler, over simmering, but not boiling, water, whisk the eggs and sugar until very thick and the whisk marks keep their shape (125°F.). Remove from the heat and fold in the chocolate. Beat in the almonds and the butter, chunk by chunk, until very smooth. Chill until the desired spreading consistency is obtained.

# Chocolate-Chestnut Torte

The sweetened chestnut purée called for in this recipe is available in tubes or cans. The cake itself—moist with a creamy, velvety texture—is a perfect ending to a glamorous Thanksgiving or Christmas dinner.

• *10 to 12 servings* •

3 ounces unsweetened chocolate
2 tablespoons (1 ounce) unsalted butter
2 tablespoons (1 ounce) water or coffee
2/3 cup (8 ounces) sweetened chestnut purée
4 large eggs, separated (1/2 cup whites, 1/3 cup yolks)
1 egg white (1/8 cup)
1/2 cup (4 ounces) sugar
1 cup (4 ounces) finely ground blanched almonds
1/4 cup (2 ounces) liqueur kirsch
Chocolate Glaze, page 85

Preheat oven to 325°F.

Butter one 9-inch round springform pan, or any pan holding 6 cups of water. Line it with wax paper, butter the paper, and flour the pan.

In the top of a double boiler, over hot, but not simmering, water, melt the chocolate. Stir in the butter, water or coffee, and chestnut purée; set aside. Beat the egg whites with 1/4 cup of the sugar until the peaks keep their shape; set aside. Beat the egg yolks with the remaining sugar until thick and ribbonlike. Fold the chocolate mixture into the beaten egg yolks. Alternately, a third at a time, fold the beaten egg whites and the almonds into the chocolate mixture. Mix only until smooth. *Do not overmix.* Pour the batter into the prepared pan and bake until a knife inserted into the center of the torte comes out clean, about 1 hour. Loosen the springform and cool 10 minutes, then gently invert onto a cooling rack. When cooled, sprinkle with liqueur kirsch and decorate with Chocolate Glaze.

# *Chocolate-Coconut Torte*

Who can resist the taste of chocolate macaroons?

• *10 to 12 servings* •

2 ounces bittersweet chocolate, grated (2/3 cup)
1 cup unsweetened coconut, grated (3 ounces)
4 large eggs, separated (1/2 cup whites, 1/3 cup yolks)
2/3 cup (5 1/2 ounces) sugar
Chocolate-Coconut Buttercream (following recipe)

Preheat oven to 325°F.

Butter two 8-inch round pans, or any pans holding 4 cups of water. Line them with wax paper, butter the paper, and flour the pans.

Mix the grated chocolate and coconut; set aside. Beat the egg whites with 1/3 cup of the sugar until the peaks keep their shape; set aside. Beat the egg yolks with the remaining 1/3 cup sugar until thick and ribbonlike. Alternately, a third at a time, fold the beaten egg whites and coconut mixture into the beaten egg yolks. Mix only until smooth. *Do not overmix.* Divide the batter equally between the prepared pans and bake until dry and a knife inserted into the center of one of the layers comes out clean, about 20 to 25 minutes. Cool 2 minutes in the pans, then gently invert onto a cooling rack. Decorate with Chocolate-Coconut Buttercream.

# *Chocolate-Coconut Buttercream*

Not too sweet, but good enough to eat by itself like candy. Form any leftovers into balls and then roll in more coconut.

• *Enough to fill and decorate one 8- to 9-inch cake* •

5 ounces bittersweet chocolate
2 tablespoons (1 ounce) coffee or water
½ cup (2 to 3 large) eggs
½ cup (4 ounces) sugar
½ cup unsweetened coconut, grated (1½ ounces)
1 cup (8 ounces) unsalted butter, at room temperature

In the top of a double boiler, over hot, but not simmering, water, melt the chocolate with the coffee or water; set aside. In the top of a double boiler, over simmering, but not boiling, water, whisk the eggs and sugar until thick and the whisk marks keep their shape (125°F.). Remove from the heat and fold in the chocolate and coconut. Beat in the butter, chunk by chunk, until very smooth. Chill until the desired spreading consistency is obtained.

# *Cocoa-Hazelnut Torte*

The distinctive flavor of hazelnuts blends well with cocoa and chocolate in this flourless torte.

• *10 to 12 servings* •

¼ cup (1 ounce) cocoa, packed
1½ cups (6 ounces) finely ground blanched hazelnuts
6 large eggs, separated (¾ cup whites, ½ cup yolks)
¾ cup (6 ounces) sugar
3 tablespoons (1½ ounces) liqueur kirsch
Chocolate Buttercream, page 82

Preheat oven to 325°F.

Butter one 9-inch round springform pan, or any pan holding 6 cups of water. Line it with wax paper, butter the paper, and flour the pan.

Sift the cocoa into the hazelnuts; set aside. Beat the egg whites with ½ cup of the sugar until the peaks keep their shape; set aside. Beat the egg yolks with the remaining ¼ cup sugar until thick and ribbonlike. Alternately, a third at a time, fold the beaten egg whites and the hazelnut mixture into the beaten egg yolks. Mix only until smooth. *Do not overmix.* Pour the batter into the prepared pan and bake until a knife inserted into the center of the torte comes out clean, about 40 minutes. Loosen the springform and cool 10 minutes, then gently invert onto a cooling rack. When cooled, sprinkle with the liqueur kirsch and decorate with Chocolate Buttercream.

# *Chocolate-Macadamia Nut Torte*

Macadamia nuts are terribly expensive, but there are those who dote on them. This *torte tropicale* is for them.

• *10 to 12 servings* •

1½ cups (6 ounces) finely chopped macadamia nuts (if salted, soak in hot water)
1 ounce bittersweet chocolate, grated (⅓ cup)
2 tablespoons (½ ounce) cocoa, packed
5 large eggs, separated (⅝ cup whites, ⅜ cup yolks)
½ cup (4 ounces) sugar
2 to 4 tablespoons (1 to 2 ounces) rum
Chocolate Buttercream, page 82

Preheat oven to 325°F.

Butter two 8-inch round pans, or any pans holding 4 cups of water each. Line them with wax paper, butter the paper, and flour the pans.

Mix the nuts and grated chocolate and sift the cocoa into them; set aside. Beat the egg whites with 1/4 cup of the sugar until the peaks keep their shape; set aside. Beat the egg yolks with the remaining 1/4 cup sugar until thick and ribbonlike. Alternately, a third at a time, fold the beaten egg whites and the nut mixture into the beaten egg yolks. Mix only until smooth. *Do not overmix.* Divide the batter equally between the prepared pans and bake until the layers start to shrink away from the sides of the pans, about 25 minutes. Cool 2 minutes in the pans, then gently invert onto a cooling rack. When cooled, sprinkle with rum and decorate with Chocolate Buttercream.

# *Pecan, Cocoa, and Coffee Torte*

This torte is made with ground, not liquid, coffee for a more intense coffee flavor. Use an espresso grind.

• *10 to 12 servings* •

2 tablespoons (1/2 ounce) cocoa, packed
1 teaspoon freshly ground coffee (not instant)
1 1/2 cups (6 ounces) finely ground pecans
4 large eggs, separated (1/2 cup whites, 1/3 cup yolks)
2/3 cup (5 1/2 ounces) sugar
2 to 4 tablespoons (1 to 2 ounces) bourbon
Bourbon and Mocha Buttercream (following recipe)
8 pecan halves or chocolate coffee bean candies

Preheat oven to 325°F.

Butter two 8-inch round pans, or any pans holding 4 cups of water each. Line them with wax paper, butter the paper, and flour the pans.

Sift the cocoa and coffee into the ground pecans; set aside. Beat the egg whites with 1/3 cup of the sugar until the peaks keep their shape; set aside. Beat the egg yolks with the remaining 1/3 cup sugar until thick and ribbonlike. Alternately, a third at a time, fold the beaten egg whites and the pecan mixture into the beaten egg yolks. Mix only until smooth. *Do not overmix.* Pour the batter into the prepared pans. Bake until dry and the layers start to shrink away from the sides of the pans, about 40 minutes. Cool 2 minutes in the pans, then gently invert onto a cooling rack. When cooled, sprinkle with the bourbon and decorate with Bourbon and Mocha Buttercream. Garnish with the pecan halves or chocolate coffee bean candies (see photograph).

# *Bourbon and Mocha Buttercream*

Bourbon and pecans are a traditional southern combination.

• *Enough to fill and decorate one 8- to 9-inch cake* •

1/4 cup (about 3 large) egg yolks
1/4 cup (2 ounces) sugar
1/4 cup (2 ounces) strong coffee
1 1/2 tablespoons (3/4 ounce) bourbon
1 cup (8 ounces) unsalted butter, very soft

In the top of a double boiler, over simmering, but not boiling, water, whisk the egg yolks, sugar, and coffee until very thick and the whisk marks keep their shape (125°F.). Remove from the heat and continue whisking. Add the bourbon when almost cool. Beat in the butter, a tablespoonful at a time. (It should be too soft to add chunk by chunk.) It is very important that the custard and butter be almost the same temperature and consistency when combined; otherwise the mixture will probably separate. The butter should look almost soupy.

# Chocolate-Pine Nut Torte

Chocolate, pine nuts, and almonds give this Italianate torte a taste almost like marzipan.

• *8 to 10 servings* •

1 ounce bittersweet chocolate, grated (1/3 cup)
3/4 cup (3 ounces) finely ground pine nuts
3/4 cup (3 ounces) finely ground almonds
4 large eggs, separated (1/2 cup whites, 1/3 cup yolks)
1/2 cup (4 ounces) sugar
1/4 cup (2 ounces) rum or liqueur kirsch
Chocolate Buttercream, page 82

Preheat oven to 325°F.

Butter two 8-inch round pans, or any pans holding 4 cups of water each. Line them with wax paper, butter the paper, and flour the pans.

Mix the chocolate and the nuts together; set aside. Beat the egg whites with 1/4 cup of the sugar until the peaks keep their shape; set aside. Beat the egg yolks with the remaining 1/4 cup sugar until thick and ribbonlike. Alternately, a third at a time, fold the beaten egg whites and the nut mixture into the beaten egg yolks. Mix only until smooth. *Do not overmix.* Divide the batter equally between the prepared pans and bake until the layers start to shrink away from the sides of the pans, about 35 minutes. Cool 2 minutes in the pans, then gently invert onto a cooling rack. When cooled, sprinkle with the rum or liqueur kirsch and decorate with Chocolate Buttercream.

# *Chocolate-Pistachio Torte*

Another flourless torte, this has an exotic and complex flavor. The pistachio nuts are tedious to prepare but are worth the trouble if you or yours are pistachio lovers.

• *8 to 10 servings* •

3/4 cup (3 ounces) finely chopped pistachio nuts
3/4 cup (3 ounces) finely ground blanched almonds
2 tablespoons (1/2 ounce) cocoa, packed
1 ounce bittersweet chocolate, grated (1/3 cup)
5 large eggs, separated (5/8 cup whites, 3/8 cup yolks)
1/2 cup (4 ounces) sugar
2 to 4 tablespoons (1 to 2 ounces) liqueur kirsch
Chocolate Buttercream, page 82, or Pistachio Buttercream, page 105

Preheat oven to 325°F.

Butter two 8-inch round pans, or any pans holding 4 cups of water each. Line them with wax paper, butter the paper, and flour the pans.

Mix the nuts, sift in the cocoa, and add the grated chocolate; set aside. Beat the egg whites with 1/4 cup of the sugar until the peaks keep their shape; set aside. Beat the egg yolks with the remaining 1/4 cup sugar until thick and ribbonlike. Alternately, a third at a time, fold the beaten egg whites and the nut mixture into the beaten egg yolks. Mix only until smooth. *Do not overmix.* Divide the batter equally between the prepared pans and bake until dry and the layers start to shrink away from the sides of the pans, about 35 minutes. Cool 2 minutes in the pans, then gently invert onto a cooling rack. Sprinkle with liqueur kirsch and decorate with Chocolate Buttercream or Pistachio Buttercream.

# *Chocolate-Walnut Torte*

Much more sophisticated than brownies, this easy, rich torte nevertheless has the same irresistible appeal.

• *10 to 12 servings* •

1¼ cups (5 ounces) finely ground walnuts
1 ounce bittersweet chocolate, grated (⅓ cup)
2 tablespoons (½ ounce) cocoa, packed
4 large eggs, separated (½ cup whites, ⅓ cup yolks)
⅔ cup (5½ ounces) sugar
Rum and Walnut Buttercream (following recipe)

Preheat oven to 325°F.

Butter two 8-inch round pans, or any pans holding 4 cups of water each. Line them with wax paper, butter the paper, and flour the pans.

Mix the walnuts with the grated chocolate and sift the cocoa into them; set aside. Beat the egg whites with ⅓ cup of the sugar until the peaks keep their shape; set aside. Beat the egg yolks with the remaining ⅓ cup sugar until thick and ribbonlike. Alternately, a third at a time, fold the beaten egg whites and the walnut mixture into the beaten egg yolks. Mix only until smooth. *Do not overmix.* Divide the batter equally between the prepared pans and bake until the layers start to shrink away from the sides of the pans and a knife inserted into the center of the layers comes out clean, about 25 minutes. Cool

2 minutes in the pans, then gently invert onto a cooling rack. When cooled, decorate with Rum and Walnut Buttercream.

# *Rum and Walnut Buttercream*

Very smooth and rich, but not too sweet.

• *Enough to fill and decorate one 8- to 9-inch cake* •

¼ cup (about 3 large) egg yolks
¼ cup (2 ounces) sugar
¼ cup (2 ounces) strong coffee
1½ tablespoons (¾ ounce) dark rum
1 cup (8 ounces) unsalted butter, very soft
¾ cup (3 ounces) finely ground toasted walnuts

In the top of a double boiler, over simmering, but not boiling, water, whisk the egg yolks, sugar, and coffee until thick and the whisk marks keep their shape (125°F.). Remove from the heat and continue whisking. Add the rum when almost cool. Beat in the butter, a spoonful at a time. (It should be too soft to add chunk by chunk.) It is very important that the custard and butter be almost the same temperature and consistency when combined; otherwise the mixture will probably separate. The butter should look almost soupy. When smooth, fold in the walnuts.

# CAKES WITH LIQUORS OR LIQUEURS

# Bourbon and Pecan Chocolate Cake

A dense, rich cake with more nuts than flour. Bourbon and pecans are a natural, and traditionally southern, flavor combination.

• *10 servings* •

4 ounces bittersweet chocolate
½ cup (4 ounces) unsalted butter
4 to 6 tablespoons (2 to 3 ounces) bourbon
3 large eggs, separated (⅓ cup whites, ¼ cup yolks)
⅔ cup (5½ ounces) sugar
⅔ cup (5½ ounces) finely ground pecans, packed
½ cup sifted and then measured (2 ounces) cake flour
Chocolate Glaze, page 85
8 pecan halves (optional)

Preheat oven to 325°F.

Butter one 8-inch round pan, or any pan holding 4 cups of water. Line it with wax paper, butter the paper, and flour the pan.

In the top of a double boiler, over hot, but not simmering, water, melt the chocolate, stirring in the butter and 2 tablespoons bourbon; set aside. Beat the egg whites with ⅓ cup of the sugar until the peaks keep their shape; set aside. Beat the egg yolks with the remaining ⅓ cup sugar until thick and ribbonlike. Blend the pecans and flour. Fold the chocolate mixture into the beaten egg yolks. Alternately, a third at a time, fold the beaten egg whites and the pecan/flour mixture into the chocolate mixture. Mix only until smooth. *Do not overmix.* Pour the batter into the prepared pan and bake until a knife inserted into the middle of the cake comes out clean, about 25 minutes. Cool 2 minutes in the pan, then gently invert onto a cooling rack. Sprinkle with 2 to 4 tablespoons bourbon and decorate with Chocolate Glaze. Place the pecan halves on top of the cake as a garnish, if desired, or write the word *Bourbon* with still-molten Chocolate Glaze (see photograph).

# *Brandy Alexander Chocolate Cake*

A rich cake with much in common with the famed after-dinner drink—plenty of brandy and cream—but with the addition of chocolate.

• *10 to 12 servings* •

4 ounces bittersweet chocolate
1/2 cup (4 ounces) unsalted butter
1/4 cup (2 ounces) brandy
1/4 cup sifted and then measured (1 ounce) cocoa
3/4 cup (3 ounces) finely ground blanched almonds
3 large eggs, separated (1/3 cup whites, 1/4 cup yolks)
1/2 cup (4 ounces) sugar

♠ ♠ ♠

3 to 5 tablespoons (1 1/2 to 2 1/2 ounces) brandy
1 1/2 cups (12 ounces) whipping cream
2 tablespoons (1 ounce) sugar
Chocolate Curls, page 69

Preheat oven to 325°F.

Butter one 9-inch round pan, or any pan holding 6 cups of water. Line it with wax paper, butter the paper, and flour the pan.

In the top of a double boiler, over hot, but not simmering, water, melt the chocolate, stirring in the butter and 1/4 cup brandy; set aside. Blend the cocoa and the almonds together; set aside. Beat the egg whites with 1/4 cup of the sugar until the peaks keep their shape; set aside. Beat the egg yolks with the remaining 1/4 cup sugar until thick and ribbonlike. Fold the chocolate mixture into the beaten egg yolks. Alternately, a third at a time, fold the beaten egg whites and the cocoa/almond mixture into the chocolate mixture. Mix only until smooth. *Do not overmix.* Pour the batter into the prepared pan and bake until a knife inserted into the center of the cake comes out clean, about 25 minutes. Cool 2 minutes in the pan, then gently invert onto a cooling rack. When cooled, sprinkle with 2 to 4 tablespoons brandy. Whip the cream with 2 tablespoons sugar and 1 tablespoon brandy. Decorate with the whipped cream and press the Chocolate Curls into the top and sides of the cake.

# *Gâteau Ivre*

Rimbaud wrote of the drunken boat, the Bateau Ivre; the Gâteau Ivre is a chocolate cake made with Drambuie.

• *8 to 10 servings* •

4 ounces bittersweet chocolate
1/2 cup (4 ounces) unsalted butter
1/4 cup (2 ounces) Drambuie
2/3 cup (4 ounces) finely ground blanched almonds, packed
1/2 cup sifted and then measured (2 ounces) cake flour
3 large eggs, separated (1/3 cup whites, 1/4 cup yolks)
1/2 cup (4 ounces) sugar

♠ ♠ ♠

2 to 4 tablespoons (1 to 2 ounces) Drambuie
Chocolate Glaze, page 85

Preheat oven to 325°F.

Butter one 8-inch round pan, or any pan holding 4 cups of water. Line it with wax paper, butter the paper, and flour the pan.

In the top of a double boiler, over hot, but not simmering, water, melt the chocolate, stirring in the butter and 1/4 cup Drambuie; set aside. Blend the almonds and the flour; set aside. Beat the egg whites with 1/4 cup of the sugar until the peaks keep their shape; set aside. Beat the egg yolks with the remaining 1/4 cup sugar until thick and ribbonlike. Fold the chocolate mixture into the beaten egg yolks. Alternately, a third at a time, fold the beaten egg whites and the almond/flour mixture into the chocolate mixture. Mix only until smooth. *Do not overmix.* Pour the batter into the prepared pan and bake until a knife inserted into the center of the cake comes out clean, about 25 minutes. Cool 2 minutes in the pan, then gently invert onto a cooling rack. Sprinkle with 2 to 4 tablespoons of Drambuie and decorate with Chocolate Glaze. With a pastry bag fitted with a writing tip, pipe the word *Ivre*, if desired.

# La Sauterelle

The Grasshopper is a cake made with chocolate and crème de menthe, another classic pairing.

• *10 to 12 servings* •

3 ounces bittersweet chocolate
2 tablespoons (1 ounce) crème de menthe
4 large eggs, separated (1/2 cup whites, 1/3 cup yolks)

½ cup (4 ounces) sugar
½ cup (2 ounces) finely ground blanched almonds

♠ ♠ ♠

1½ cups (12 ounces) whipping cream
1 tablespoon (½ ounce) sugar
1 tablespoon (½ ounce) crème de menthe
Chocolate Curls, page 69

Preheat oven to 325°F.

Butter two 8-inch round pans, or any pans holding 4 cups of water cach. Line them with wax paper, butter the paper, and flour the pans.

In the top of a double boiler, over hot, but not simmering, water, melt the chocolate, stirring in 2 tablespoons of crème de menthe; set aside. Beat the egg whites with ¼ cup sugar until the peaks keep their shape; set aside. Beat the egg yolks with the remaining ¼ cup sugar until thick and ribbonlike. Fold the chocolate into the beaten egg yolks. Alternately, a third at a time, fold the beaten egg whites and the almonds into the chocolate mixture. Mix only until smooth. *Do not overmix.* Pour the batter into the prepared pans and bake until a knife inserted into the center of the cakes comes out clean, about 20 to 25 minutes. Cool 2 minutes in the pans, then gently invert onto a cooling rack.

Whip the cream with the 1 tablespoon of sugar and 1 tablespoon of crème de menthe. Decorate the cake with the whipped cream and press the Chocolate Curls into the top and sides of the cake.

# *Kahlúa Chocolate Cake*

Coffee and chocolate have been a popular combination for centuries, and no wonder.

• *10 to 12 servings* •

6 ounces bittersweet chocolate
1/2 cup (4 ounces) unsalted butter
4 tablespoons (2 ounces) Kahlúa or Coffee Liqueur, page 103
1/2 cup sifted and then measured (2 ounces) cake flour
3/4 cup (5 ounces) finely ground blanched almonds, packed
3 large eggs, separated (1/3 cup whites, 1/4 cup yolks)
2/3 cup (5 1/2 ounces) sugar
2 tablespoons (1 ounce) liqueur kirsch
Chocolate Glaze, page 85

Preheat oven to 325°F.

Butter one 9-inch round pan, or any pan holding 6 cups of water. Line it with wax paper, butter the paper, and flour the pan.

In the top of a double boiler, over hot, but not simmering, water, melt the chocolate, stirring in the butter and 2 tablespoons of Kahlúa or Coffee Liqueur; set aside. Blend the flour and the almonds; set aside. Beat the egg whites with 1/3 cup of the sugar until the peaks keep their shape; set aside. Beat the egg yolks with the remaining 1/3 cup sugar until thick and ribbonlike. Fold the chocolate mixture into the beaten egg yolks. Alternately, a third at a time, fold the beaten egg whites and the flour/almond mixture into the chocolate mixture. Mix only until smooth. *Do not overmix.* Pour the batter into the prepared pan and bake until a knife inserted into the center of the cake comes out clean, about 25 minutes. Cool 2 minutes in the pan, then gently invert onto a cooling rack. When cooled, sprinkle with the Kahlúa or Coffee Liqueur and liqueur kirsch, and decorate with Chocolate Glaze.

# *Maraschino Chocolate Cake*

A fudgy confection for grown-ups, this cake has double chocolate and cherry liqueur

• *10 to 12 servings* •

8 ounces bittersweet chocolate
1/3 cup (2 1/2 ounces) unsalted butter
4 tablespoons (2 ounces) maraschino
1/2 cup sifted and then measured (2 ounces) cake flour
1/2 cup (3 ounces) finely ground blanched almonds, packed
3 large eggs, separated (1/3 cup whites, 1/4 cup yolks)
2/3 cup (5 1/2 ounces) sugar
2 tablespoons (1 ounce) liqueur kirsch
Chocolate Glaze, page 85

Preheat oven to 325°F.

Butter one 9-inch round pan, or any pan holding 6 cups of water. Line it with wax paper, butter the paper, and flour the pan.

In the top of a double boiler, over hot, but not simmering, water, melt the chocolate, stirring in the butter and 2 tablespoons of maraschino; set aside. Blend the flour and almonds; set aside. Beat the egg whites with 1/3 cup of the sugar until the peaks keep their shape; set aside. Beat the egg yolks with the remaining 1/3 cup sugar until thick and ribbonlike. Fold the chocolate mixture into the beaten egg yolks. Alternately, a third at a time, fold the beaten egg whites and the flour/almond mixture into the chocolate mixture. Mix only until smooth. *Do not overmix.* Pour the batter into the prepared pan and bake until a knife inserted into the center of the cake comes out clean, about 40 to 45 minutes. Cool 15 minutes in the pan, then gently invert onto a cooling rack. When cooled, sprinkle the cake with the remaining 2 tablespoons of maraschino and the liqueur kirsch, and decorate with Chocolate Glaze.

# Rum and Chocolate Cake

This cake improves with 1 or 2 days of aging, the rum and chocolate blending into a richer and more complex flavor.

• *10 to 12 servings* •

6 ounces bittersweet chocolate
½ cup (4 ounces) unsalted butter
4 to 6 tablespoons (2 to 3 ounces) dark rum
¾ cup (6 ounces) finely ground blanched almonds, packed
½ cup sifted and then measured (2 ounces) cake flour
3 large eggs, separated (⅓ cup whites, ¼ cup yolks)
⅔ cup (5½ ounces) sugar
Chocolate Glaze, page 85

Preheat oven to 325°F.

Butter one 8-inch round pan, or any pan holding 4 cups of water. Line it with wax paper, butter the paper, and flour the pan.

In the top of a double boiler, over hot, but not simmering, water, melt the chocolate, stirring in the butter and 2 tablespoons rum; set aside. Blend the almonds and flour; set aside. Beat the egg whites with 1/3 cup of the sugar until the peaks keep their shape; set aside. Beat the egg yolks with the remaining 1/3 cup sugar until thick and ribbonlike. Fold the chocolate mixture into the beaten egg yolks. Alternately, a third at a time, fold the beaten egg whites and the almond/flour mixture into the chocolate mixture. Mix only until smooth. *Do not overmix.* Pour the batter into the prepared pan and bake until a knife inserted into the center of the cake comes out clean, about 30 minutes. Cool 2 minutes in the pan, then gently invert onto a cooling rack. When cooled, sprinkle with 2 to 4 tablespoons rum and decorate with Chocolate Glaze.

# Rum Raisin Chocolate Cake

As a child, my favorite ice cream flavor was rum raisin, which always surprised adults who thought no child could like rum. Chocolate only adds to the near-perfect rum-raisin duet.

• *10 to 12 servings* •

1/4 cup (2 ounces) dark rum
1/2 cup (3 1/2 ounces) chopped raisins, packed
6 ounces bittersweet chocolate
1/2 cup (4 ounces) unsalted butter
4 large eggs, separated (1/2 cup whites, 1/3 cup yolks)
1/2 cup (4 ounces) sugar
1 cup sifted and then measured (4 ounces) cake flour
Chocolate Glaze, page 85

Pour the rum over the raisins and allow them to steep for 30 minutes.

Preheat oven to 325°F.

Butter one 9-inch round pan, or any pan holding 6 cups of water. Line it with wax paper, butter the paper, and flour the pan.

In the top of a double boiler, over hot, but not simmering, water, melt the chocolate, stirring in the butter and raisins; set aside. Beat the egg whites with 1/4 cup of the sugar until the peaks keep their shape; set aside. Beat the egg yolks with the remaining 1/4 cup sugar until thick and ribbonlike. Fold the chocolate mixture into the beaten egg yolks. Alternately, a third at a time, fold the beaten egg whites and the flour into the chocolate mixture. Mix only until smooth. *Do not overmix.* Pour the batter into the prepared pan and bake until a knife inserted into the middle of the cake comes out clean, about 30 minutes. Cool 2 minutes in the pan, then gently invert onto a cooling rack. When cooled, decorate with Chocolate Glaze.

# *Whiskey Chocolate Cake*

As this cake needs no refrigeration and is fairly dense, it travels well and is good for picnics. It is a brownie for adults.

• *10 to 12 servings* •

4 ounces bittersweet chocolate
1/2 cup (4 ounces) unsalted butter
6 to 8 tablespoons (3 to 4 ounces) whiskey
1/2 cup (3 ounces) finely ground blanched hazelnuts, packed
2/3 cup sifted and then measured (2 1/2 ounces) cake flour
3 large eggs, separated (1/3 cup whites, 1/4 cup yolks)
2/3 cup (5 1/2 ounces) sugar
Chocolate Glaze, page 85

Preheat oven to 325°F.

Butter one 9-inch round pan, or any pan holding 6 cups of water. Line it with wax paper, butter the paper, and flour the pan.

In the top of a double boiler, over hot, but not simmering, water, melt the chocolate, stirring in the butter and 4 tablespoons whiskey; set aside. Blend the hazelnuts and the flour; set aside. Beat the egg whites with ⅓ cup of the sugar until the peaks keep their shape; set aside. Beat the egg yolks with the remaining ⅓ cup sugar until thick and ribbonlike. Fold the chocolate mixture into the beaten egg yolks. Alternately, a third at a time, fold the beaten egg whites and the hazelnut/flour mixture into the chocolate mixture. Mix only until smooth. *Do not overmix*. Pour the batter into the prepared pan and bake until a knife inserted into the center of the cake comes out clean, about 30 minutes. Cool 2 minutes in the pan, then gently invert onto a cooling rack. When cooled, sprinkle the cake with 2 to 4 tablespoons whiskey and decorate with Chocolate Glaze.

# MOLDED CAKES

# Black Hole Cake

A cake with the icing in the middle rather than on the outside. Although you need a special pan, the cake is so good the pan is worth purchasing. Children love the "tunnel" of fudgy icing. A 2-hour setting time is required before serving.

• *8 to 10 servings* •

¾ cup (3 to 4 large) eggs
¾ cup (6 ounces) granulated sugar
1½ cups sifted and then measured (6 ounces) cake flour
¾ cup (6 ounces) unsalted butter, melted

♠ ♠ ♠

½ cup sifted and then measured (2 ounces) cocoa
1 cup sifted and then measured (4 ounces) confectioners' sugar
3 tablespoons (1½ ounces) unsalted butter
½ cup (4 ounces) whipping cream

♠ ♠ ♠

¼ cup (2 ounces) Grand Marnier or rum (optional)
Confectioners' sugar

Preheat oven to 325°F.

Butter and flour one 13-inch-long and 2½-inch-deep "Deerback" or "Rehrruchen" pan or any similar pan holding 5 cups of water.

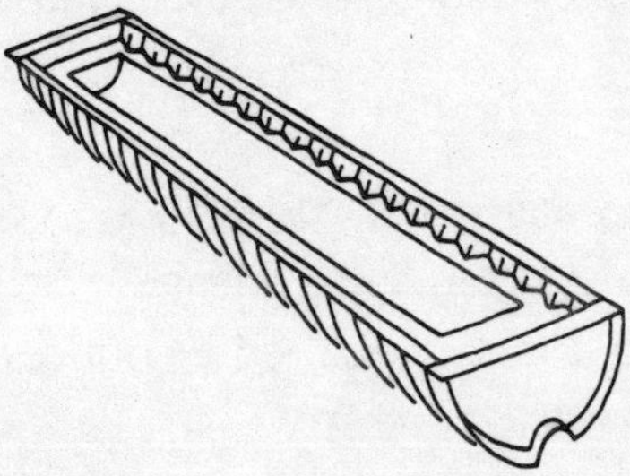

Whisk the eggs and granulated sugar in a mixing bowl over simmering, but not boiling, water until they are too hot to keep a finger in for more than a second (125°F.). Remove from the heat and beat with an electric mixer until very thick and ribbonlike. Gently fold in the flour while trickling in the melted butter. Mix only until smooth. *Do not overmix.* Pour the batter into the prepared pan and bake until a knife inserted into the center of the cake comes out clean, about 25 minutes. Cool 2 minutes in the pan, then gently invert onto a cooling rack. When cooled, return to the pan. Scoop out a cavity about 1 inch deep and 2 inches wide, leaving a rim around the entire cake. Save the scooped-out portion for crumbs (page 52).

In a heavy saucepan, bring the cocoa, 1 cup confectioners' sugar, butter, and cream to a boil, stirring constantly. Lower the heat, and simmer for 5 minutes, stirring occasionally. Cool until the bottom of the saucepan is not too hot to touch, otherwise the fudge will be absorbed into the cake ½ inch and look sloppy.

Sprinkle the Grand Marnier or rum over the cake, if desired. Pour the cooled fudge into the cavity of the cake and refrigerate until set, about 2 hours. Invert the cake onto a serving platter and sprinkle with confectioners' sugar.

# *Bûche de Noël*

The Bûche de Noël, or "Yule Log," is a French chocolate roll that is traditionally served after midnight mass on Christmas Eve.

• *12 servings* •

4 large eggs, separated (½ cup whites, ⅓ cup yolks)
½ cup (4 ounces) granulated sugar
¾ cup sifted and then measured (3 ounces) cake flour
Mousse au Chocolat, page 91

¼ cup (2 ounces) brandy or cognac (optional)
Chocolate Buttercream, page 82
Meringue Mushrooms (following recipe) or marzipan mushrooms
Confectioners' sugar

Preheat oven to 325°F.

Butter one 12-by-18-inch baking sheet. Line it with wax paper, butter the paper, and flour the sheet.

Beat the egg whites with ¼ cup of the granulated sugar until the peaks keep their shape; set aside. Beat the egg yolks with the remaining ¼ cup granulated sugar until thick and ribbonlike. Alternately, a third at a time, fold the beaten egg whites and the flour into the beaten egg yolks. Mix only until smooth. *Do not overmix.* Spread the batter evenly onto the prepared sheet and bake until slightly set but not crisp, about 12 to 15 minutes. Sprinkle with granulated sugar and roll up with the wax paper *immediately* upon taking it out of the oven. Cool, then unroll very gently. Spread the chocolate mousse evenly over the unrolled cake. Roll it up again, this time peeling off the wax paper.

Cut off both ends of the rolled cake in parallel diagonals. Place these ends on top of the cake to simulate wood knots. Sprinkle with

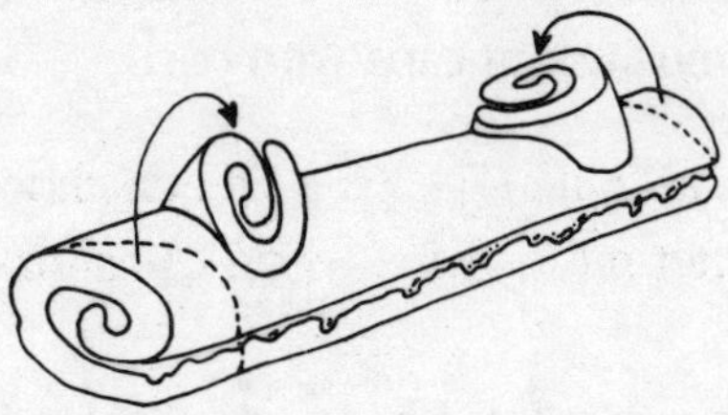

the brandy or cognac, if desired. Decorate with Chocolate Buttercream, using a fork to simulate the texture of bark. Garnish with Meringue or marzipan Mushrooms. Immediately before serving, sprinkle with confectioners' sugar to simulate snow (see photograph).

# *Meringue Mushrooms*

These decorative confections can be made a week or two ahead of time before the last-minute Christmas rush. Store well sealed.

• *About 12* •

1 egg white
Sugar
1 tablespoon Chocolate Buttercream, page 82
Cocoa

Preheat oven to 275°F.

Butter and sprinkle with sugar one 12-by-18-inch baking sheet lined with wax paper.

Measure the egg white and then measure out a double amount of sugar. Beat the egg white and sugar until *very* stiff. Place the mixture in a pastry bag fitted with a ½-inch nozzle tip. Pipe strips ½ to ¾ inch long for the mushroom stems and 1 to 1½ inches round for the mushroom caps. Bake 1 to 1½ hours, or until very dry. Peel away from the paper and store in an airtight box. Before placing the mushrooms on the Bûche de Noël, dab a little Chocolate Buttercream on the underside of the cap. Press the stem against the buttercream as glue. Sprinkle the mushroom caps with cocoa.

# *Chocolate Charlotte*

Although this cake is spectacular, it is not very difficult. The recipe can be undertaken in stages and at one's leisure, since there are many components. A 4-hour setting time is required before serving.

*16 servings*

16 Ladyfingers, page 80, heavily sprinkled with liqueur kirsch

♠ ♠ ♠

1 tablespoon unflavored gelatin
1 cup (8 ounces) whipping cream
1 tablespoon (½ ounce) sugar
3 tablespoons (1½ ounces) liqueur kirsch
1 cup Crème Pâtissière au Chocolat, page 119
2 ounces bittersweet chocolate, grated (⅔ cup)

♠ ♠ ♠

1 Génoise Simple, page 78

♠ ♠ ♠

½ cup (4 ounces) whipping cream
2 teaspoons sugar
1 teaspoon liqueur kirsch

♠ ♠ ♠

Chocolate Curls, page 69, or 12 rosebuds

Butter an 8-inch brioche mold or any bowl 8 inches wide and 3 inches deep. Arrange the ladyfingers to cover the bottom and sides of the brioche mold. Pack them together as tightly as possible.

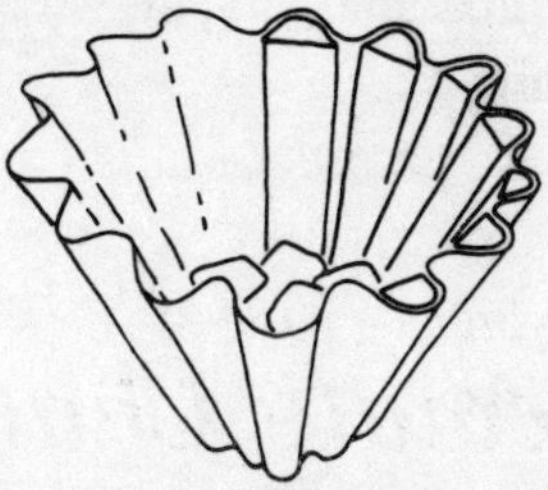

In a small saucepan, mix the gelatin with 2 tablespoons whipping cream. Allow the mixture to sit for 5 minutes, or until it looks very grainy. Place the remainder of the cup of cream, 1 tablespoon sugar, and 3 tablespoons liqueur kirsch in a mixing bowl and have an electric mixer ready. Over a low heat, melt the gelatin, stirring constantly to prevent scorching. *Immediately* pour the gelatin into the cream and whip it until it almost turns to butter. Fold the Crème Pâtissière au Chocolat and the grated chocolate into the whipped cream. Adjust the amounts of sugar and liqueur kirsch if necessary. Pour the mixture into the ladyfinger-lined mold. Wrap securely and refrigerate until set, about 4 hours.

At serving time, loosen the charlotte by placing the mold in a bowl of hot water for a few seconds. Place the génoise on top of the mold, trim if necessary, and invert onto the serving platter.

Whip ½ cup cream, 2 teaspoons sugar, and 1 teaspoon liqueur kirsch, and put it in a pastry bag fitted with a star tip. Pipe a decorative pattern over the top and sides of the charlotte (see photograph). Garnish with Chocolate Curls or rosebuds.

# *Chestnut, Pear, and Chocolate Charlotte*

As with the Chocolate Charlotte (preceding recipe), this creation is better undertaken in stages, as it has many components. It is equally spectacular and a truly great midwinter dessert. A 4-hour setting time is required before serving.

• *12 to 16 servings* •

16 Chocolate Ladyfingers, page 81, heavily sprinkled with liqueur kirsch

♠ ♠ ♠

2 large (16 ounces) underripe Anjou pears
1 cup (8 ounces) sugar
1 cup (8 ounces) water

♠ ♠ ♠

1 tablespoon (½ ounce) unflavored gelatin
1 tablespoon (½ ounce) cold water
3 ounces unsweetened chocolate
1 cup Crème Pâtissière, page 118
⅔ cup (8 ounces) chestnut purée, sweetened (available in cans and tubes)
2 tablespoons (1 ounce) liqueur kirsch
½ cup (4 ounces) cream, whipped

♠ ♠ ♠

1 Génoise au Chocolat, page 78

♠ ♠ ♠

½ cup (4 ounces) whipping cream
2 teaspoons sugar
1 teaspoon liqueur kirsch

♠ ♠ ♠

Chocolate Curls, page 69, or chocolate chestnut bonbons

Butter an 8-inch brioche mold or any bowl 8 inches wide and 3 inches deep.

Arrange the ladyfingers to cover the bottom and sides of the brioche mold. Pack them together as tightly as possible.

Peel, halve, and core the pears. In a heavy saucepan, dissolve 1 cup sugar in 1 cup water. Bring to a boil and add the pears. Turn the heat down to a simmer and cook, covered, until the pears are soft, about 20 minutes. Drain the pears on a rack and dice.

In a small saucepan, dissolve the gelatin in 1 tablespoon water. Allow the gelatin to sit for 5 minutes, or until it looks grainy. In the top of a double boiler, over hot, but not simmering, water, melt the chocolate. Over low heat, melt the gelatin, stirring constantly to prevent scorching. *Immediately* pour the gelatin into the Crème Pâtissière and stir until blended. Fold the chocolate, chestnut purée, pears, 2 tablespoons liqueur kirsch, and whipped cream into the crème. Adjust the amounts of sugar and liqueur kirsch, if necessary.

Pour the mixture into the ladyfinger-lined mold. Wrap securely and refrigerate until set, about 4 hours.

At serving time, loosen the charlotte by placing the mold in a bowl of hot water for a few seconds. Place the génoise on top of the mold, trim it if necessary, and invert onto the serving platter.

Whip ½ cup cream, 2 teaspoons sugar, and 1 teaspoon liqueur kirsch, and put it in a pastry bag fitted with a star tip. Pipe a decorative pattern over the top and sides of the charlotte (see photograph). Garnish with Chocolate Curls, or chocolate chestnut bonbons.

# Rum and Chocolate Charlotte

This cake is the most fabulous-looking of all the charlottes. A 4-hour setting time is required before serving.

• *10 to 12 servings* •

1 Bûche de Noël, page 184, filled with Mousse au Chocolat, page 91, but not decorated with Chocolate Buttercream

♠ ♠ ♠

1 tablespoon (½ ounce) unflavored gelatin
1 tablespoon (½ ounce) cold water
6 ounces bittersweet chocolate
1 cup Crème Pâtissière, page 118
¼ cup (2 ounces) dark rum
1 cup (8 ounces) cream, whipped

♠ ♠ ♠

½ cup (4 ounces) whipping cream
1 teaspoon sugar
1 teaspoon dark rum

♠ ♠ ♠

Chocolate Curls, page 69

Line with plastic a bowl 8 inches wide and 4 inches deep, or any bowl holding 7 cups of water.

Place the Bûche de Noël in the freezer to facilitate slicing. When partially frozen, slice into ½-inch segments. Arrange the segments along the bottom and sides of the plastic-lined bowl, reserving 6 to 8 slices for the top.

In a small saucepan, dissolve the gelatin in the water. Allow the mixture to sit for 5 minutes, or until it looks very grainy. In the top of a double boiler, over hot, but not simmering, water, melt the chocolate. Over low heat, melt the gelatin, stirring constantly to prevent scorching. *Immediately* pour the gelatin into the Crème Pâtissière and stir until blended. Fold the chocolate, ¼ cup rum, and the whipped cream into the crème. Pour the mixture into the cake-lined mold and arrange the remaining pieces over the top. Wrap securely and refrigerate until set, about 4 hours.

Gently invert the charlotte onto the serving platter by pulling off the plastic. Whip ½ cup cream, the sugar, 1 teaspoon rum. Place the whipped cream in a pastry bag fitted with a star tip. Pipe a decorative pattern around the bottom of the charlotte. Garnish with Chocolate Curls.

# Croquembouches au Chocolat

*Croquembouches* translates as "crunchy mouthfuls." It is a tower of carolines (cream puffs) and looks very impressive.

• *10 to 15 servings* •

2 cups (16 ounces) water
1 cup (8 ounces) salted butter
2 cups sifted and then measured (8 ounces) plain flour
2 cups (8 to 9 large) eggs

♠ ♠ ♠

1 cup (8 ounces) cream, whipped
2 cups Crème Pâtissière au Chocolat, page 119

♠ ♠ ♠

Chocolate Glaze, page 85

Preheat oven to 375°F.

Line two 12-by-18-inch baking sheets with wax paper and butter the paper.

In a heavy saucepan, boil the water and butter. Remove from the heat and add the flour all at once, beating until smooth. Add the eggs in four additions and beat vigorously. Immediately put this mixture in a pastry bag fitted with a ½-inch nozzle tip. Pipe 48 balls (carolines) 1½ inches in diameter. Bake until the carolines are golden and

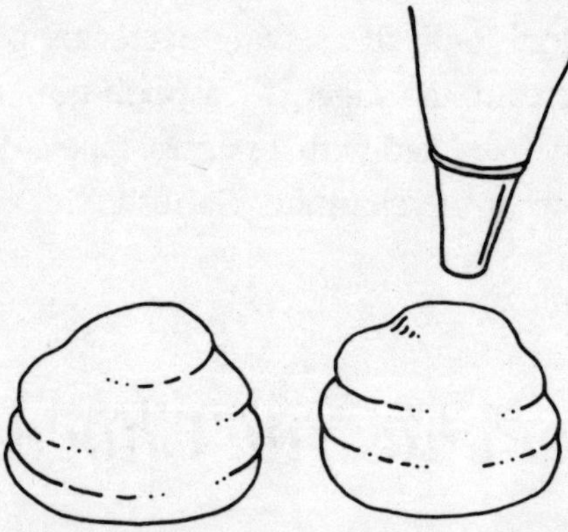

seem to sweat, about 30 minutes. Reduce the oven heat to 275°F. and bake another 30 minutes. If the carolines seem completely dry and hollow, remove them from the oven. Otherwise, turn the oven off and leave the carolines in until they are completely dry.

Fold the whipped cream and Crème Pâtissière au Chocolat together. Place the mixture in a pastry bag fitted with a ½-inch nozzle tip. Pierce each caroline on the underside with a knife. Pipe the cream mixture into each caroline. Dip each caroline halfway into the Chocolate Glaze. Assemble the cake by arranging 12 carolines in a circle to form the bottom ring, chocolate glaze side down. Arrange 8 to 9 carolines on top of the bottom ring, converging toward the center (use chocolate glaze as glue if necessary). Continue building the cake with converging rings. Exercise extreme caution lest the cake collapse. Serve immediately.

# *Gâteau St. Honoré au Chocolat*

This cake is intended for the virtuoso exhibitionist, not the beginning *chef pâtissier*. It is a veritable summation of a pastry-maker's art, combining pâte au choux, pâte feuilletée, crème pâtissière, and crème chantilly (cream puffs, puff pastry, pastry cream, and whipped cream).

• *8 to 10 servings* •

1/4 teaspoon salt
3 tablespoons (1 1/2 ounces) water
1/4 cup (4 ounces) unsalted butter
1 cup sifted and then measured (4 ounces) pastry flour; or 3/4 cup sifted and then measured (3 ounces) plain flour and 1/4 cup sifted and then measured (1 ounce) cake flour

♠ ♠ ♠

1/2 cup (4 ounces) water
1/4 cup (2 ounces) salted butter
1/2 cup sifted and then measured (2 ounces) plain flour
1/2 cup (2 to 3 large) eggs

♠ ♠ ♠

2 cups Crème Pâtissière au Chocolat, page 119
1 cup (8 ounces) cream, whipped

♠ ♠ ♠

1/4 recipe Chocolate Glaze, page 85

Preheat oven to 400°F. when the pastry is ready to be baked.

Line one 12-by-18-inch baking sheet with wax paper. Butter and flour the paper.

Dissolve the salt in 3 tablespoons water and place in the freezer until very cold but not icy. Mix 2 tablespoons of the unsalted butter with the pastry flour until the mixture resembles peas. Pour the icy water into the flour mixture all at once and mix until smooth. Do not knead like a bread dough. Pat the dough into a rectangle, wrap securely, and refrigerate 2 hours. Form the remaining butter into a rectangle 3 by 4 inches, ½ inch thick. Refrigerate until "leather-hard." (The butter should bend like leather, not snap.)

Roll the dough out on a lighly floured board into a rectangle 7 by 8 inches, ¼ inch thick. Place the remaining unsalted butter on the center of the dough and fold the sides of the dough over it to form a

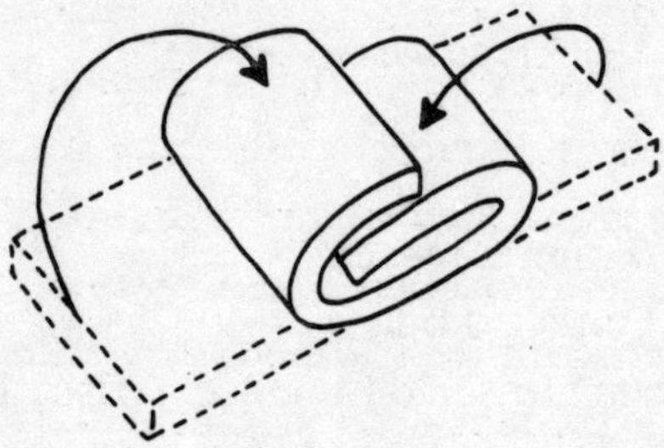

sealed envelope. Pound the dough with a rolling pin to make the rolling easier. Roll the dough out to a ¼-inch thickness. Fold a third of the dough back on itself, forming 2 plys, and then fold the remaining third back on the 2 plys to form 3 plys. For maximum efficiency, exert force directly perpendicular to the dough and roll from the center outward, not back and forth. Flour the board only if necessary to prevent the dough from sticking and tearing. Dust off excess flour, as it could cause the dough to become tough. Repeat the rolling and folding procedure for a total of six times. The rolling and folding can be done in sets of two. Refrigerate 30 minutes between two sets of rolling and folding. Allow the dough to rest in the refrigerator at least 3 hours or overnight after the folding is done.

Roll the dough out to make a circle 9 inches in diameter. Gently flap the dough to relax it, the same way one would flap a beach towel to get rid of sand. Trim the edges with a sharp knife to form a circle. Do not drag the knife lest the layering effect be compromised. Cover the dough circle with plastic and refrigerate 30 minutes.

In a heavy saucepan, bring 1 cup water and the salted butter to a boil. Remove from the heat and add ½ cup all-purpose flour all at once, beating until smooth. Add the eggs and beat vigorously. Immediately, put this choux mixture in a pastry bag fitted with a ½-inch nozzle tip. Pipe 12 balls (carolines) 1 inch in diameter onto the prepared baking sheet. Place the puff pastry circle on the same baking sheet and pipe the remaining choux mixture around the edge of the circle to form a rim. Bake until the carolines are golden and seem to sweat, about 20 to 25 minutes. Remove the carolines from the oven and cool on a rack away from drafts. Continue baking the puff pastry circle until it is golden brown, about 15 to 20 minutes more. Cool thoroughly on the sheet and transfer to a serving platter.

Pierce each caroline with a knife on the underside. Fold the Crème Pâtissière au Chocolat and whipped cream together. Place the mixture in a pastry bag fitted with a ¼-inch nozzle tip. Inject the mixture into each caroline. Pipe the remaining mixture into the center well of the puff pastry circle.

Dip each caroline halfway into the glaze and arrange them chocolate side up on top of the rim. Dribble any remaining glaze onto the cream in the center. Serve immediately.

# *Poupelin au Chocolat*

This cake resembles a great big cream puff.

• *6 to 8 servings* •

¾ cup (6 ounces) water
6 tablespoons (3 ounces) salted butter
¾ cup sifted and then measured (3 ounces) plain flour
3 large (about ⅔ cup) eggs

♠ ♠ ♠

1 cup (8 ounces) whipping cream
1 tablespoon (½ ounce) liqueur kirsch
4 ounces bittersweet chocolate, grated (1⅓ cups)
Sugar to taste (optional)

♠ ♠ ♠

2 ounces bittersweet chocolate
¼ cup (2 ounces) unsalted butter

Preheat oven to 375°F.

Line one 8-inch pan with wax paper. Butter the paper and sides of the pan generously.

In a heavy saucepan, boil the water and salted butter. Remove from the heat and add the flour all at once, beating until smooth. Add the eggs and beat vigorously. Spread the mixture into the prepared pan and bake until golden and the cake seems to sweat, about 30 minutes. Reduce the oven heat to 275°F. and bake another 30 minutes. If the cake seems dry and hollow, remove it from the oven. Otherwise, turn the oven off and leave the cake in until it seems completely dry. Cool on a rack, away from drafts.

Whip the cream with the liqueur kirsch. Fold in the grated chocolate. Add sugar, if desired. Place the whipped cream in a pastry bag fitted with a ½-inch nozzle tip. Pierce the underside of the poupelin with a knife. With the cake inverted, pipe the cream into the cake.

In the top of a double boiler, over hot, but not simmering, water, melt the 2 ounces chocolate, stirring in the unsalted butter. Pour over the poupelin. Serve when the glaze has set.

# *Chocolate Roll*

Very simple, but impressive, and a favorite with almost everyone.

• *8 to 10 servings* •

6 ounces bittersweet chocolate
3 tablespoons (1½ ounces) water or coffee
5 large eggs, separated (⅝ cup whites, ⅜ cup yolks)
½ cup (4 ounces) sugar
½ cup (2 ounces) finely ground unblanched almonds

♠ ♠ ♠

1 cup (8 ounces) whipping cream
1 tablespoon (½ ounce) sugar
1 teaspoon liqueur kirsch (optional)
Cocoa
Confectioners' sugar

Preheat oven to 350°F.

Butter one 12-by-18-inch baking sheet. Line it with wax paper, butter the paper, and flour the pan.

In the top of a double boiler, over hot, but not simmering, water, melt the chocolate with the water or coffee; set aside. Beat the egg whites with ¼ cup of the sugar until the peaks still fall over; set aside. Beat the egg yolks with the remaining ¼ cup of sugar until just creamy. Stir the chocolate and the almonds into the beaten egg yolks. Fold the beaten egg whites into the chocolate mixture. Spread evenly into the prepared pan and bake until set, but not dry on top, about 20 minutes. Remove from the oven and cover with a damp cloth. Cool for 20 minutes, then gently remove the cloth. Sprinkle the cloth with cocoa. Invert the cake onto the cloth gently and peel away the wax paper.

Whip the cream with 1 tablespoon sugar and the liqueur kirsch, if desired. Spread the whipped cream over the cake. Roll the cake over onto itself by grasping the cloth, not touching the cake. Transfer the roll to a serving platter or board and dust with additional cocoa or confectioners' sugar.

# *Swiss Chocolate Roll*

A spongy chocolate jelly-roll.

• *8 to 10 servings* •

5/8 cup sifted and then measured (2½ ounces) cake flour
2 tablespoons (½ ounce) cocoa, packed
4 large eggs, separated (½ cup whites, ⅓ cup yolks)
½ cup (4 ounces) granulated sugar
1½ cups (18 ounces) jelly, jam, or marmalade
Confectioners' sugar

Preheat oven to 325°F.

Butter one 12-by-18-inch baking sheet. Line it with wax paper, butter the paper, and flour the pan.

Sift the flour and cocoa together twice; set aside. Beat the egg whites with ¼ cup granulated sugar until the peaks keep their shape;

set aside. Beat the egg yolks with the remaining ¼ cup granulated sugar until thick and ribbonlike. Alternately, a third at a time, fold the flour/cocoa mixture and the beaten egg whites into the beaten egg yolks. Mix only until smooth. *Do not overmix.* Spread the batter evenly into the prepared pan and bake until dry and set but not crisp, about 12 minutes. Sprinkle the cake with granulated sugar and roll it up with the wax paper *immediately* upon taking it out of the oven. Cool, then unroll very gently. Spread the jelly, jam, or marmalade over the unrolled cake. Roll it up again, this time peeling off the wax paper. Sprinkle with confectioners' sugar before serving.

# UNIQUE CAKES

# Black Bottom Pie

An authentic recipe from Mississippi, this pie is made with a crumb crust, a layer of chocolate on the bottom, a filling of whiskey-flavored custard, and a topping of whipped cream and chocolate curls. A setting time of 4 hours is required before serving.

• *8 to 10 servings* •

½ cup (4 ounces) unsalted butter, melted
1½ cups (6 ounces) cake crumbs

♠ ♠ ♠

1 tablespoon (½ ounce) unflavored gelatin
1 tablespoon (½ ounce) cold water
2 cups (16 ounces) milk
½ cup (4 ounces) sugar
1 tablespoon cornflour
4 large eggs, separated (½ cup whites, ⅓ cup yolks)
¼ cup (2 ounces) whiskey
2 ounces bittersweet chocolate, grated (⅔ cup)

♠ ♠ ♠

½ cup (4 ounces) whipping cream
1 tablespoon (½ ounce) sugar
1 teaspoon whiskey

♠ ♠ ♠

Chocolate Curls, page 69

Preheat oven to 325°F.

Use one 9-inch springform pan; no buttering required.

Mix the butter and crumbs and press them evenly into the pan. Bake 15 minutes. Cool.

Dissolve the gelatin in the water; set aside. In the top of a double boiler, over simmering, but not boiling, water, place the milk. In a bowl, mix ½ cup sugar and the cornflour, and whisk in the egg yolks. Pour the yolk mixture into the milk and cook, whisking constantly, until thick and shiny. Remove from the heat and add ¼ cup whiskey. Remove 1 cup of the custard and stir the grated chocolate into it. Pour this chocolate mixture into baked crust. Add the gelatin to the remaining hot custard and whisk until the gelatin has dissolved. Beat the egg whites until stiff but not dry. Fold them into the custard and pour it over the chocolate mixture. Chill until set, about 4 hours.

At serving time, whip the cream with 1 tablespoon sugar and 1 teaspoon whiskey and place it in a pastry bag fitted with a star tip. Pipe a decorative border around the edge of the pie. Pile the Chocolate Curls on top of the rest of the pie.

# Boston Cream Pie

Not a pie at all, but a chocolate cake. The women at Radcliffe used to sneak a piece of this cake to their rooms when it was served in their dormitories.

• *8 to 10 servings* •

One 8-inch Génoise Simple, page 78
½ cup Crème Pâtissière, page 118
Chocolate Glaze, page 85

Split the génoise into 2 layers with a serrated knife. Spread the crème on the bottom layer and assemble the other layer on top of it. Decorate with Chocolate Glaze.

# Chocolate Beet Torte

Your guests will never guess the featured ingredient of this torte. The beetroots lose their vegetable character and take on a mild sweetness that complements the walnuts and chocolate. At least 2 days are required for aging.

• *12 to 16 servings* •

4 small beetroots, peeled
1½ cups (6 ounces) finely ground walnuts
¼ cup sifted and then measured (1 ounce) cake flour
4 ounces bittersweet chocolate
5 large eggs, separated (⅝ cup whites, ⅜ cup yolks)
¾ cup (6 ounces) sugar
2 to 4 tablespoons (1 to 2 ounces) Grand Marnier (optional)
Chocolate Glaze, page 85

Preheat oven to 325°F.

Butter one 9-inch round pan, or any pan holding 6 cups of water. Line it with wax paper, butter the paper, and flour the pan.

Grate the beetroots onto a cloth towel. Press the excess moisture out of them. Measure 1 cup beetroots and mix the walnuts and flour into them; set aside. In the top of a double boiler, over hot, but not simmering, water, melt the chocolate; set aside. Beat the egg whites with ¼ cup of the sugar until the peaks keep their shape; set aside. Beat the egg yolks with the remaining ½ cup sugar until thick and ribbon-like. Fold the chocolate into the beaten egg yolks. Alternately, a third at a time, fold the beaten egg whites and beet-walnut mixture into the chocolate mixture. Mix only until smooth. *Do not overmix.* Pour the batter into the prepared pan and bake until a knife inserted in the center of the cake comes out clean, about 1 hour. Do not be alarmed at the starchy smell when the torte is taken from the oven—it will mellow. Cool 10 minutes in the pan, then gently invert onto a cooling rack. Place a cardboard support under the cake and wrap securely. Refrigerate at least 2 days to age.

Sprinkle the Grand Marnier on the torte, if desired, and decorate with Chocolate Glaze.

# *Chocolate Carrot Torte*

This is the best carrot cake I've ever tasted!

• *12 to 16 servings* •

2 large carrots
1½ cups (6 ounces) finely ground walnuts
¼ cup sifted and then measured (1 ounce) cake flour
4 ounces bittersweet chocolate, grated (1⅓ cups)
½-inch cinnamon stick, ground, or ½ teaspoon ground cinnamon
5 large eggs, separated (⅝ cup whites, ⅜ cup yolks)
¾ cup (6 ounces) sugar
2 to 4 tablespoons (1 to 2 ounces) liqueur kirsch (optional)
Chocolate Glaze, page 85

Preheat oven to 325°F.

Butter one 9-inch round pan, or any pan holding 6 cups of water. Line it with wax paper, butter the paper, and flour the pan.

Peel and grate the carrots. Measure 1 cup of the grated carrots with the walnuts, flour, chocolate, and cinnamon; set aside. Beat the egg whites with ½ cup of the sugar until the peaks keep their shape; set aside. Beat the egg yolks with the remaining ¼ cup sugar until thick and ribbonlike. Alternately, a third at a timc, fold the beaten egg whites and the carrot mixture into the beaten egg yolks. Mix only until smooth. *Do not overmix.* Pour the batter into the prepared pan and bake until a knife inserted into the center comes out clean, about 1 to 1½ hours. Cool 10 minutes in the pan, then gently invert onto a cooling rack. Sprinkle with the liqueur kirsch, if desired, and decorate with Chocolate Glaze.

# Chocolate Potato Torte

Based on a traditional recipe from the Portuguese Azores, this torte keeps exceptionally well.

• *10 to 12 servings* •

1 large potato
1½ cups (6 ounces) finely ground walnuts
6 ounces bittersweet chocolate, grated (2 cups)
2 pinches freshly ground nutmeg
1 pinch freshly ground cinnamon
4 large eggs, separated (½ cup whites, ⅓ cup yolks)
1 cup (8 ounces) sugar
½ cup (4 ounces) unsalted butter
Chocolate Glaze, page 85

Preheat oven to 325°F.

Butter one 9-inch round pan, or any pan holding 6 cups of water. Line it with wax paper, butter the paper, and flour the pan.

Boil the unpeeled potato until soft, about 10 to 20 minutes. Cool thoroughly, then peel and rice. Measure 1 cup of the riced potato and mix with the walnuts, chocolate, nutmeg, and cinnamon; set aside. Beat the egg whites with 1/2 cup of the sugar until the peaks keep their shape; set aside. Beat the egg yolks with the remaining 1/2 cup of sugar until ribbonlike. Alternately, a third at a time, fold the beaten egg whites and the potato mixture into the beaten egg yolks. Mix only until smooth. *Do not overmix.* Pour the batter into the prepared pan and bake until a knife inserted into the center of the torte comes out clean, about 40 minutes. Cool 10 minutes in the pan, then gently invert onto a cooling rack. Decorate with Chocolate Glaze.

# *Chocolate Courgette Torte*

Courgettes are almost endlessly versatile, although few would expect them to turn up in a chocolate cake. They add to the torte's moistness as would a fruit. At least 2 days is required for aging.

• *12 to 16 servings* •

3 small courgettes
1 1/2 cups (6 ounces) finely ground walnuts
1/4 cup sifted and then measured (1 ounce) cake flour
4 ounces bittersweet chocolate
5 large eggs, separated (5/8 cup whites, 3/8 cup yolks)
3/4 cup (6 ounces) sugar
Chocolate Glaze, page 85

Preheat oven to 325°F.

Butter one 9-inch round pan, or any pan holding 6 cups of water. Line it with wax paper, butter the paper, and flour the pan.

Wash and grate the courgettes onto a cloth towel. Press the excess moisture out of them. Measure 1 cup of the grated courgettes and mix it with the walnuts and flour. In the top of a double boiler, over hot, but not simmering, water, melt the chocolate; set aside. Beat the egg whites with ½ cup of the sugar until the peaks keep their shape; set aside. Beat the egg yolks with the remaining ¼ cup sugar until thick and ribbonlike. Fold the chocolate into the beaten egg yolks. Alternately, a third at a time, fold the beaten egg whites and courgette mixture into the chocolate mixture. Mix only until smooth. *Do not overmix*. Pour the batter into the prepared pan and bake until a knife inserted into the center of the cake comes out clean, about 1 hour. Do not be alarmed at the starchy smell when the torte is taken from the oven—it will mellow. Cool 10 minutes in the pan, then gently invert onto a cooling rack. Place a cardboard support under the cake and wrap securely. Refrigerate at least 2 days for aging. Decorate with Chocolate Glaze.

# *Chocolate Biscuit Torte*

This recipe is based on a traditional Spanish cake. The biscuits, or ladyfingers, are soaked with coffee and become almost puddinglike. A 1-hour setting time is required before serving.

• *6 to 8 servings* •

20 Chocolate Ladyfingers, baked until dry and brittle, 1½ recipe, page 81
1 cup strong coffee (laced with Kahlúa or Coffee Liqueur, page 103, if desired)
Cocoa Kahlúa Buttercream, page 103
1 cup (4 ounces) chopped walnuts

Place the coffee in a shallow baking pan or plate with a rim. Soak each ladyfinger in it. On the serving platter, arrange 3 or 4 ladyfingers (enough to make a square) for a bottom layer. Spread a thin layer of

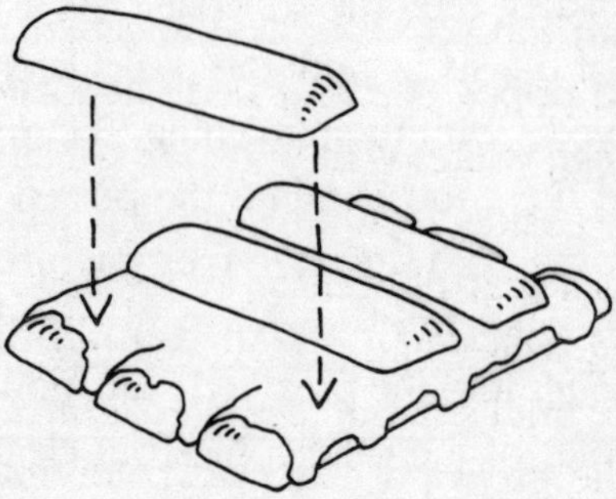

buttercream over the ladyfingers. Repeat until all the ladyfingers are used. There should be 5 or 6 layers. Spread the remaining buttercream on the top and sides of the cake and press the walnuts into the buttercream. Refrigerate at least 1 hour before serving.

# Chocolate-Poppy Seed Torte

Usually relegated to the realm of garnishes, poppy seeds, which are delightfully sweet, are the featured element of this torte.

• *10 to 12 servings* •

1 cup (6 ounces) poppy seeds
2 ounces bittersweet chocolate, grated (⅔ cup)
2 pinches freshly ground cinnamon
4 large eggs, separated (½ cup whites, ⅓ cup yolks)
⅔ cups (5½ ounces) sugar
2 to 4 tablespoons (1 to 2 ounces) liqueur kirsch (optional)
Chocolate Buttercream, page 82

Preheat oven to 325°F.

Butter two 8-inch round pans, or any pans holding 4 cups of water each. Line them with wax paper, butter the paper, and flour the pans.

Mix together the poppy seeds, grated chocolate, and cinnamon; set aside. Beat the egg whites with 1/3 cup of the sugar until the peaks keep their shape; set aside. Beat the egg yolks with the remaining 1/3 cup sugar until thick and ribbonlike. Alternately, a third at a time, fold the beaten egg whites and poppy-seed mixture into the beaten egg yolks. Mix only until smooth. *Do not overmix.* Divide the batter equally between the prepared pans and bake until dry and a knife inserted into the center comes out clean, about 20 to 25 minutes. Cool 2 minutes in the pan, then gently invert onto a cooling rack. When cooled, sprinkle with liqueur kirsch, if desired, and decorate with Chocolate Buttercream.

# *Cocoa Ginger Cake*

Molasses gives this slightly spicy cake its dark color, while cocoa imparts a chocolaty taste.

• *10 to 12 servings* •

1 cup sifted and then measured (4 ounces) cake flour
2 tablespoons (1/2 ounce) cocoa, packed
1 teaspoon powdered ginger
4 large eggs, separated (1/2 cup whites, 1/3 cup yolks)
1 cup (8 ounces) granulated sugar
1/3 cup (4 ounces) dark molasses
6 tablespoons (3 ounces) unsalted butter, at room temperature

♠ ♠ ♠

1/4 cup (2 ounces) Grand Marnier
1 cup (8 ounces) whipping cream
2 tablespoons (1 ounce) granulated sugar
Confectioners' sugar

Preheat oven to 325°F.

Butter two 8-inch round pans, or any pans holding 4 cups of water each. Line them with wax paper, butter the paper, and flour the pans.

Sift the flour, cocoa, and ginger together twice; set aside. Beat the egg whites with 1 cup granulated sugar until the peaks keep their shape; set aside. Beat the egg yolks with the molasses and butter until very smooth. Alternately, a third at a time, fold the beaten egg whites and the flour into the beaten egg yolks. Mix only until smooth. *Do not overmix.* Pour the batter into the prepared pans and bake until a knife inserted into the center of the cakes comes out clean, about 20 to 25 minutes. Cool 2 minutes in the pans, then gently invert onto a cooling rack.

When cool, split each layer into 2 with a serrated knife. Sprinkle each layer with 1 tablespoon Grand Marnier. Whip the cream with 2 tablespoons granulated sugar. Assemble the layers with whipped cream between them. Sprinkle the cake with confectioners' sugar.

# Doboshtorte

A Hungarian specialty, Doboshtorte is a seven-layer cake composed of six somewhat dry spongy cake layers and a seventh of caramel. It is a handsome creation.

• *8 to 10 servings* •

3 large eggs, separated (1/3 cup whites, 1/4 cup yolks)
3/8 cup (3 ounces) sugar
1/2 cup sifted and then measured (2 ounces) cake flour

♠ ♠ ♠

6 tablespoons (3 ounces) rum or liqueur kirsch
Chocolate Buttercream, page 82
1 cup (4 ounces) finely ground blanched hazelnuts

♠ ♠ ♠

1/2 cup (4 ounces) sugar

Preheat oven to 325°F.

Butter a 12-by-18-inch baking sheet (jelly-roll pan). Line it with wax paper, butter the paper, and flour the pan.

Beat the egg whites with 1/4 cup sugar until the peaks keep their shape; set aside. Beat the egg yolks with the remaining 1/8 cup sugar until thick and ribbonlike. Alternately, a third at a time, fold the beaten egg whites and the flour into the beaten egg yolks. Mix only until smooth. *Do not overmix.* Spread the batter evenly over the prepared pan and bake until slightly golden and set, but not crispy, about 15 minutes.

*Immediately* upon taking the cake from the oven, cut it in half crosswise so there are two 9-by-12-inch layers. Cut each of these layers into thirds crosswise to obtain six 4-by-9-inch layers. Sprinkle each layer with 1 tablespoon rum or liqueur kirsch. Spread Chocolate Buttercream on 5 of the layers and assemble the layers with the undecorated one on top. Trim the sides of the cake with a serrated knife and decorate the top and sides with the remaining Chocolate Buttercream. Press the hazelnuts into the buttercream on the sides of the cake.

Draw a rectangle 4 by 10 inches on a piece of wax paper or parchment (not all brands of wax paper produce successful results; use parchment paper, available in specialty stores, if your brand of wax paper does not work). Divide the rectangle into ten 1-by-4-inch rectangles. Turn the paper over and butter it generously. In a heavy saucepan, melt the sugar over a low heat, stirring as it browns. When

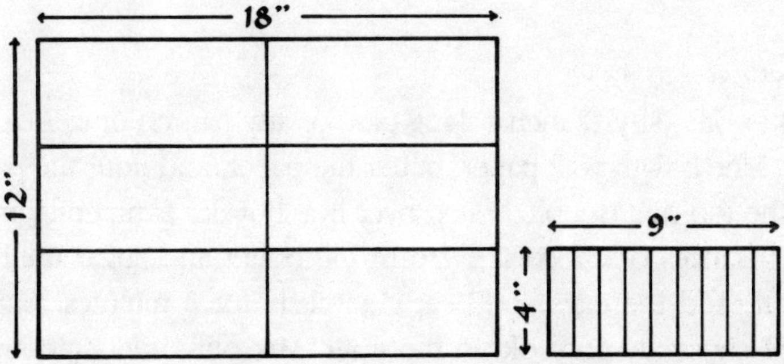

the sugar reaches a rich caramel color, remove from the heat and pour it onto the buttered paper. When slightly cooled, cut ten 1-by-4-inch pieces, following the pencil marks on the underside. Discard the excess caramel. Be extremely careful not to burn yourself when handling the hot sugar. When cooled, peel the caramel away from the paper and place on top of the cake (see photograph).

Do not be discouraged if the caramel is not successful at the first attempt. This is a very failure-prone operation, as even the virtuosos will admit.

# *Double Chocolate Brownies*

These fudgelike little cakes are topped with even more chocolate. Perhaps the ultimate brownie.

• *10 to 12 servings* •

7 ounces bittersweet chocolate
6 tablespoons (3 ounces) unsalted butter, very soft
3/4 cup (6 ounces) sugar
3 large (3/4 cup) eggs
3/4 cup sifted and then measured (3 ounces) plain flour
6 ounces bittersweet chocolate, grated (2 cups)

Preheat oven to 325°F.

Butter one 8-by-12-inch baking pan, or any pan holding 7 cups of water. Line it with wax paper, butter the paper, and flour the pan.

In the top of a double boiler, over hot, but not simmering, water, melt 7 ounces of chocolate. Cream the butter and sugar until very smooth. Add the eggs and beat vigorously for 2 minutes. Add the melted chocolate and fold in the flour. Mix only until smooth. *Do not overmix.* Pour into the prepared pan and bake until a knife inserted into the center comes out clean, about 25 minutes.

Immediately upon removing the brownies from the oven, sprinkle on the grated chocolate. When it has melted, spread it evenly. When cooled and the top chocolate has hardened, cut into 20 squares with a serrated knife.

# *Honey Brownies*

Very easy, these little honey cakes stay fresh for several days.

• *8 to 16 servings* •

3 ounces unsweetened chocolate
3/8 cup (3 ounces) unsalted butter
3/4 cup (9 ounces) honey
3 large (3/4 cup) eggs
3/4 cup (6 ounces) granulated sugar
3/4 cup sifted and then measured (3 ounces) plain flour
3/4 cup (3 ounces) chopped walnuts, raisins, or mixture
Confectioners' sugar

Preheat oven to 325°F.

Butter one 8-by-12-inch baking pan, or any pan holding 7 cups of water. Line it with wax paper, butter the paper, and flour the pan.

In the top of a double boiler, over hot, but not simmering, water, melt the chocolate, stirring in the butter and honey; set aside. Beat the eggs with the granulated sugar until very thick. Alternately, a third at a time, fold the chocolate mixture and the flour into the beaten eggs. Mix only until smooth. *Do not overmix.* Pour the batter into the prepared pan and bake until a knife inserted into the center comes out clean, about 35 minutes. Cool in the pan. Place a doily on the brownies and sprinkle confectioners' sugar through it. Cut into 16 squares.

# *Molé Cake*

Molé tastes similar to the drink made by the Aztecs with cacao. This is a main-course "chocolate cake." An aging period of 2 to 3 days is required for the sauce.

• *6 to 8 servings* •

2 pounds turkey or chicken bones

♠ ♠ ♠

1/4 cup blanched almonds
2 tablespoons sesame seeds
2 flour tortillas
1/2 bulb garlic, minced
3 small onions, chopped
5 large tomatoes, diced
1/4 cup oil (olive, sesame, or combination)
3 hot peppers (jalapeño, Anaheim, and/or chili)
2 teaspoons freshly ground cinnamon
1 teaspoon freshly ground cloves
1 teaspoon aniseed
1/2 teaspoon ground coriander

♠ ♠ ♠

2 ounces unsweetened chocolate, grated
2 to 3 tablespoons (1 1/2 to 2 ounces) honey
Juice of 1 lime
Salt

♠ ♠ ♠

12 flour tortillas
3 pounds cooked turkey, boned and diced
2 cups cooked rice
½ pound jack cheese, or other mild cheese, grated

♠ ♠ ♠

3 cups chopped lettuce
1 avocado, thinly sliced

Make a stock by simmering the turkey or chicken bones with water to cover for 2 to 3 hours. Pour through a strainer and refrigerate until the fat sets on top and may be discarded.

Toast the almonds, sesame seeds, and 2 tortillas 5 minutes under a broiler. Grind in a blender or food processor; set aside. Sauté the garlic, onions, and tomatoes in the oil and add the peppers and spices. Stir in the ground mixture. In a large saucepan or stockpot, place 2 to 3 cups of the stock and the mixture. Simmer, uncovered, for 2 hours. Cover and refrigerate 2 to 3 days to age. To serve, heat the sauce and add the chocolate, honey, and lime juice. Adjust the salt.

On an oiled baking sheet or in a 12-inch round pan, place a tortilla. Layer some turkey, rice, cheese, and molé sauce over the tortilla. Repeat until all the tortillas are used, ending with a tortilla. Reserve the remaining molé sauce. Bake the cake until heated throughout, about 25 to 30 minutes. Serve smothered with the remaining sauce. Garnish with the chopped lettuce and avocado slices.

# Othello Petits Fours

One of the family of petits fours including Desdemonas (white for purity), Iagos (green for jealousy), and Rosamundas (pink for roses).

• *25 petits fours* •

5/8 cup sifted and then measured (2 1/2 ounces) cake flour
2 tablespoons (1/2 ounce) cocoa, packed
4 large eggs, separated (1/2 cup whites, 1/3 cup yolks)
1/2 cup (4 ounces) sugar
1/4 cup (2 ounces) brandy or liqueur kirsch
1/2 cup (4 ounces) apricot jam
Chocolate Glaze, page 85
25 whole blanched almonds

Preheat oven to 325°F.

Butter one 12-by-18-inch baking sheet. Line it with wax paper, butter the paper, and flour the pan.

Sift the flour and cocoa together twice; set aside. Beat the egg whites with 1/4 cup of the sugar until the peaks keep their shape; set aside. Beat the egg yolks with the remaining 1/4 cup sugar until thick and ribbonlike. Alternately, a third at a time, fold the beaten egg whites and flour/cocoa into the beaten egg yolks. Mix only until smooth. *Do not overmix.* Spread the batter evenly into the prepared pan and bake until set, about 12 to 15 minutes. Cool on the sheet.

Cut the cake, including the wax paper, into two 9-by-12-inch

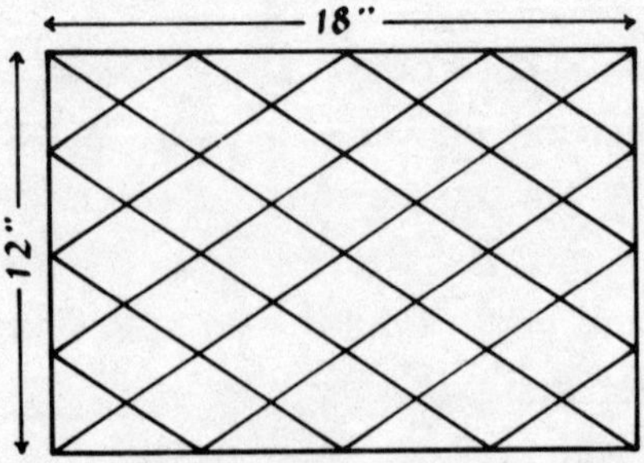

pieces. Sprinkle the brandy or liqueur kirsch on the layers. Spread the jam on one layer and assemble the other layer on top of it, wax paper side up. Put in the freezer to facilitate cutting. When almost frozen, peel away the wax paper from both sides and slice into diamond shapes. Decorate with Chocolate Glaze and garnish each petit four with a whole blanched almond.

# *Soufflé au Chocolat*

Not strictly a cake, but one of the finest of all chocolate creations. It lacks flour or nuts, yet how could it be omitted? As with all soufflés, this must be served immediately.

• *6 servings* •

¼ cup (2 ounces) unsalted butter
2 tablespoons (½ ounce) cocoa, packed
1 cup (8 ounces) whipping cream
3 ounces bittersweet chocolate
½ cup (4 ounces) granulated sugar
5 large eggs, separated (⅝ cup whites, ⅜ cup yolks)
Confectioners' sugar

Preheat oven to 350°F.

Butter and sprinkle with sugar one 8-inch soufflé dish holding 8 cups of water.

Melt the butter and stir in the cocoa; set aside. In a heavy saucepan, combine the cream, chocolate, and granulated sugar. Heat until the chocolate melts. Stir the butter and cocoa into the egg yolks and add to the cream mixture. Remove from the heat. Beat the egg whites until stiff and fold them into the other ingredients. Pour the batter into the prepared pan and bake until dry and set, about 25 minutes. Sprinkle with confectioners' sugar and serve immediately.

# *Torta Sorentina*

A traditional Italian Easter cake, Torta Sorentina is made in a tube pan, split into 3 layers, filled with chocolate buttercream, soaked with Grand Marnier, and glazed with chocolate. *Fabuloso!*

• *8 to 10 servings* •

1 cup (8 ounces) unsalted butter
1 cup (4 to 5 large) eggs
1 cup (8 ounces) sugar
2 cups sifted and then measured (8 ounces) cake flour
½ teaspoon grated lemon or orange rind
¼ cup (2 ounces) Grand Marnier
½ recipe Chocolate Buttercream, page 82
Chocolate Glaze, page 85
¼ cup Candied Citrus Rind, page 129

Preheat oven to 325°F.

Butter a Savarin mold or any tubular pan holding 6 cups of water.

Melt the butter; set aside. Whisk the eggs and sugar in a mixing bowl over hot, but not boiling, water, until they reach body temperature, about 100°F. Remove from the heat and beat with an electric mixer until very thick, about 5 minutes. Gently fold in the flour and grated rind while trickling in the butter. Mix only until smooth. *Do not overmix.* Pour the batter into the prepared pan and bake until a knife inserted into the center of the cake comes out clean, about 25 minutes. Cool 2 minutes in the pan, then gently invert onto a cooling rack.

When cooled, split the cake into 3 layers with a serrated knife. Sprinkle each layer with Grand Marnier. Spread the Chocolate Buttercream between the layers. Spread any remaining buttercream on the sides of the cake to make it perfectly smooth. Refrigerate until the buttercream has hardened. Decorate with Chocolate Glaze and garnish with Candied Citrus Rind. (See photograph.)

# Triple Chocolate Cheese Cake

This is not a subtle cake, but it is rich, dense, and delicious. At least a 12-hour setting time is required before serving.

• *12 to 16 servings* •

½ cup (4 ounces) unsalted butter, melted
2 cups (8 ounces) chocolate cake crumbs

♠ ♠ ♠

2 ounces bittersweet chocolate
2 tablespoons (1 ounce) Grand Marnier or coffee
2 tablespoons (½ ounce) cocoa, packed
1 cup (8 ounces) sugar
1 cup (4 to 5 large) eggs
1 pound cream cheese, at room temperature

♠ ♠ ♠

4 ounces bittersweet chocolate
⅓ cup (2½ ounces) sour cream

Use one 9-inch springform pan; no buttering required.

Mix the butter with the crumbs and press them evenly into the pan. Wrap and freeze or place in the refrigerator overnight.

In the top of a double boiler, over hot, but not simmering, water, melt 2 ounces chocolate with the Grand Marnier or coffee; set aside. Sift the cocoa into the sugar. Blend the chocolate, sugar, cocoa, eggs, and cream cheese until smooth. *Do not overmix.* The cheese cake will crack in the oven if it is overmixed. To achieve a foolproof result, refrigerate the batter overnight to relax it.

Preheat oven to 325°F. At baking time, pour the batter into the pan and bake until all but the center inch of the cake is set, about 1 hour. The center inch will set as the cake cools.

In the top of a double boiler, over hot, but not simmering, water, melt 4 ounces chocolate, stirring in the sour cream. Spread it on top of the cake. Wrap and refrigerate at least 12 hours before slicing.

# *Pain au Chocolat*

These little pastries filled with chocolate are wonderful for a special breakfast or for tea.

• *15 little pastries* •

2 teaspoons yeast
2 tablespoons (1½ ounces) honey
2½ cups sifted and then measured (10 ounces) plain flour
½ cup (4 ounces) milk
2 large (½ cup, scant) eggs
1 teaspoon salt
¼ cup (2 ounces) unsalted butter, at room temperature

♠ ♠ ♠

15 ounces bittersweet chocolate

♠ ♠ ♠

1 egg

Line a 12-by-18-inch baking sheet with wax paper. Butter the paper.

Mix the yeast, honey, and a handful of the flour into the milk. Set aside 10 to 15 minutes, or until the mixture looks foamy and smells yeasty. Add the eggs, salt, and half the remaining flour. Add the butter chunk by chunk and mix until it is completely blended. Add the rest of the flour and mix until very smooth. Knead on a floured board until silky, about 5 minutes. (This dough is very sticky.) Cover securely and refrigerate at least 4 hours or overnight.

Divide the dough into 15 pieces, about 1½ ounces each. Form each piece into a ball and roll it out into a square or rectangle ¼ inch thick. Place 1 ounce chocolate in the center of each dough square. Fold the dough around the chocolate to form a little envelope. Pinch to seal. Place, pinched side down, on the baking sheet 1 inch apart.

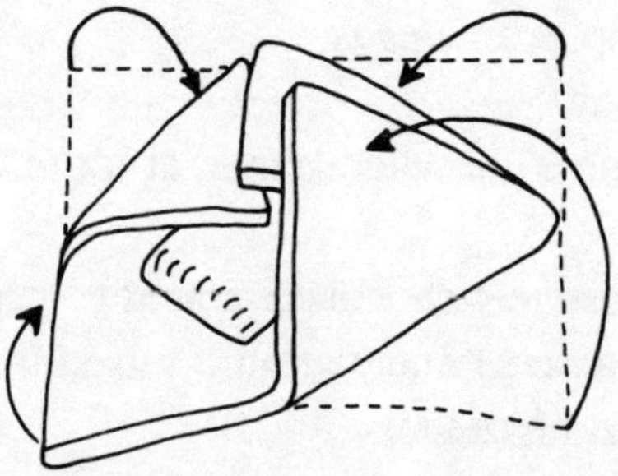

Cover with damp cloth or plastic and allow to rise until the dough feels very moist and spongy, about 1 hour.

Preheat oven to 350°F. Beat the egg slightly and brush each little pastry with it. Bake until golden, about 15 to 20 minutes. Cool on a rack.

# Chocolate and Three-Nut Coffee Cake

A yeast bread that is perfect for a festive brunch.

• *8 to 10 servings* •

1 tablespoon yeast (dry granulated or moist cake yeast)
¼ cup ( 3 ounces) honey
5 cups sifted and then measured (20 ounces) plain flour
1 cup (8 ounces) milk, at room temperature
2 large (½ cup, scant) eggs
2 teaspoons salt
½ cup (4 ounces) unsalted butter, at room temperature

♠ ♠ ♠

3 ounces bittersweet chocolate, grated (1 cup)
1½ cups (6 ounces) finely ground mixed nuts: walnuts, almonds, and hazelnuts
2-inch cinnamon stick, ground, or 1 teaspoon ground cinnamon
½ cup (4 ounces) sugar
Water or honey (¼ to ½ cup; enough to make a paste)

♠ ♠ ♠

1 egg

Generously butter a 9-inch round pan, or any pan holding 6 cups of water.

Mix the yeast, honey, and a handful of the flour into the milk. Set aside 10 to 15 minutes, or until the mixture looks foamy and smells yeasty. Add 2 eggs, salt, and half the remaining flour. Add the butter chunk by chunk and mix until it is completely blended. Add the rest of the flour and mix until very smooth. Knead on a floured board until silky, about 5 minutes. (This dough is very sticky.) Cover securely and refrigerate at least 4 hours or overnight.

Roll out a quarter of the dough on a floured board into a circle 14 inches in diameter, ¼ inch thick. Stretch this dough circle into the prepared pan folding the excess over like a pastry shell. Roll the remaining dough into a rectangle about 8 by 12 inches, ¼ inch thick.

Mix the chocolate, nuts, cinnamon, and sugar. Add enough water or honey just to make a paste. Spread a quarter of the nut mixture over the dough circle bottom. Spread the remaining nut mixture over the rectangle. Roll up the rectangle lengthwise. Cut it into 1-inch segments. Place these segments on top of the dough circle, cut side up.

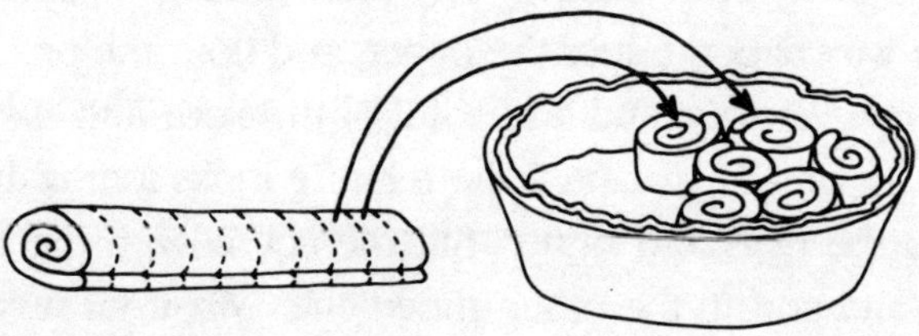

Cover and allow to rise in a warm place until the dough feels very moist and spongy, about 1 hour, or place the covered coffee cake to rise in the refrigerator overnight. The next day preheat the oven to 350°F. Beat egg slightly and brush the risen coffee cake with it. Bake until golden and the bottom of the cake sounds hollow when briskly tapped, about 45 minutes. Cool on a rack.

# *Yeasted Chocolate Cake*

A marvelous coffee cake to serve for a brunch dessert or almost anytime. It is somewhat tart with an unusual chocolaty flavor.

• *10 to 12 servings* •

1 tablespoon yeast
½ cup (6 ounces) honey
2½ cups sifted and then measured (10 ounces) plain flour
½ cup (4 ounces) milk, at room temperature
2 large (½ cup, scant) eggs, at room temperature
½ cup (4 ounces) unsalted butter, melted
½ cup sifted and then measured (2 ounces) cocoa
Chocolate Honey Glaze I or II, page 94

Butter one 9-inch round pan, or any pan holding 6 cups of water. Line it with wax paper, butter the paper, and flour the pan.

Mix the yeast, honey, and a handful of the flour into the milk. Set aside 10 to 15 minutes, or until the mixture looks foamy and smells yeasty. Add the eggs and butter. Sift the cocoa with the remaining flour twice and add to the other ingredients. Mix until very smooth. Cover securely and refrigerate overnight.

The next day, spread the dough into the prepared pan and allow it to rise in a warm place until the dough has doubled in bulk and is very soft and spongy, about 1 hour.

Preheat oven to 325°F. Bake until a knife inserted in the center of the cake comes out clean, about 30 minutes. Cool 2 minutes in the pan, then gently invert onto a cooling rack. Decorate with Chocolate Honey Glaze.

# · WEIGHT/VOLUME · · EQUIVALENCY CHART ·

*Butter:* 1 cup = 8 ounces
*Chocolate, grated:* 1 cup, not packed = 3 ounces
*Cocoa:* 1 cup, packed = 4 ounces
*Cocoa:* 1 cup, sifted and measured = 3 ounces
*Cocoa:* 1 tablespoon, packed = 1/4 ounce
*Cocoa:* 2 tablespoons, packed = 1/2 ounce
*Cocoa:* 1/3 cup, sifted and measured = 1 ounce
*Coconut:* 1 cup, not packed = 3 ounces
*Coconut:* 1 cup, packed = 4 ounces
*Eggs:* whole, 1 cup = 4 to 5 large
*Egg whites:* 1 cup = 8 to 9 large
*Egg yolks:* 1 cup = 12 to 13 large
*Flour (any and all):* 1 cup, sifted and measured = 4 ounces
*Honey:* 1 cup liquid (not crystallized) = 12 ounces
*Jam, jelly, and preserves:* 1 cup = 12 ounces
*Liquid (liqueur, coffee, etc.):* 1 cup = 8 ounces
*Nuts (finely ground, unblanched, not very oily):* 1 cup (not packed) = 4 ounces
*Nuts (finely ground, blanched):* 1 cup, packed = 8 ounces
*Nuts (finely ground, unblanched, very oily, e.g., pecans, and some hazelnuts):* 1 cup, packed = 6 ounces
*Sugar, granulated:* 1 cup = 8 ounces
*Sugar, powdered (confectioners'):* 1 cup, sifted and measured = 4 ounces
*Sugar, brown:* 1 cup, packed = 8 ounces

NOTE: For all ingredients for purposes of simplicity, when 1 cup = 8 ounces, 1/3 cup = 2 1/2 ounces, and 2/3 cup = 5 1/2 ounces.

# OVEN TEMPERATURES AND CONVERSION TABLES

## OVEN TEMPERATURES

| *Gas* | *Electric* °F |
|---|---|
| Low | 200 |
| 1/4 | 225 |
| 1/2 | 250 |
| 1 | 275 |
| 2 | 300 |
| 3 | 325 |
| 4 | 350 |
| 5 | 375 |
| 6 | 400 |
| 7 | 425 |
| 8 | 450 |
| 9 | 475 |

## METRIC CONVERSION

| | |
|---|---|
| 1 oz = 25 g | 1 fl oz = 28.4 ml |
| 2 oz = 50g | 1/4 pint = 150 ml |
| 4 oz = 100 g | 1/2 pint = 300 ml |
| 8 oz = 225 g | 1 pint = 600 ml |
| 1 lb = 450 g | 35 fl oz = 1 litre |

## CUP MEASUREMENTS

1 British Standard Cup = 10 fl oz or ½-pint
1 US Standard Cup = 8 fl oz or US ½-pint

| | *British Standard Cup* | *American Standard Cup* |
|---|---|---|
| Flour | 5 oz | 4 oz |
| Sugar – Granulated, Castor or Superfine | 9 oz | 8 oz |
| Icing or Confectioners' Sugar | 5 oz | 4½ oz |
| Butter/Lard/Margarine | 9 oz | 8 oz |

## MEASURING SPOONS

American measuring spoons are smaller than British measuring spoons.

| | *British Spoon (level)* | *American Spoon (level)* |
|---|---|---|
| Sifted flour | 3 tablespoons = 1 oz | 4 tablespoons = 1 oz |
| Sugar – Granulated, Castor or Superfine | 2 tablespoons = 1¼ oz | 2 tablespoons = 1 oz |
| Icing or Confectioners' Sugar (sifted) | 3 tablespoons = 1 oz | 4 tablespoons = 1 oz |
| Butter/Margarine | 2 tablespoons = 1¼ oz | 2 tablespoons = 1 oz |
| Rice | 2 tablespoons = 1¼ oz | 2 tablespoons = 1 oz |
| Cornflour | 2 tablespoons = 1 oz | 3 tablespoons = 1 oz |
| Syrup/Treacle | 1 tablespoon = 1 oz | 1 tablespoon = ¾ oz |
| Gelatine – powdered or granulated | 4 teaspoons = ½ oz | 5 teaspoons = ½ oz |

# • INDEX •

Pamella Asquith is the author of *The Quintessential Croissant* and *Pamella Z. Asquith's Fruit Tart Cookbook*. She has worked as a professional cook, baker, and pastry chef and lives in Berkeley, California.